Cultural Globalization and Plurality

CULTURAL GLOBALIZATION AND PLURALITY

AFRICA AND THE NEW WORLD

Abdul-Rasheed Na'Allah

AFRICA WORLD PRESS
TRENTON | LONDON | CAPE TOWN | NAIROBI | ADDIS ABABA | ASMARA | IBADAN

AFRICA WORLD PRESS
541 West Ingham Avenue | Suite B
Trenton, New Jersey 08638

Copyright © 2011 Abdul-Rasheed Na'Allah
First Printing 2011

Book and cover design: Saverance Publishing Services

Library of Congress Cataloging-in-Publication Data

Na'allah, Abdul Rasheed.
  Cultural globalization and plurality Africa and the new world / by Abdul-Rasheed Na'allah.
    p. cm.
  Includes bibliographical references and index.
    ISBN 1-59221-720-6 -- ISBN 1-59221-721-4 (pbk.) 1. Culture diffusion--Africa. 2. Pluralism--Africa. 3. Globalization. I. Title.
  DT16.5.N33 2010
  303.48'2607--dc22

                        2010002091

For

Milan V. Dimić and Marguerite Garstin

(my late teachers and friends in Edmonton, Alberta, Canada,
theirs was,
a wedlock of the gods!)

Table of Contents

Acknowledgments
꿔꿩

A work like this cannot represent a single person's scholarly ingenuity. Indeed, most of the stories and scholarly citations and arguments I respond to in this book belong to others—communities, ancestors, living elders, scholarly peers—and I acknowledge all those before me upon whose shoulders I stand. I must also acknowledge my friends and academic colleagues in Nigeria, Canada, and the United States, as many of the book's discussions have involved their participation in one form or the other. I am grateful to the many students at different levels of education in Canada (particularly in Edmonton, Alberta) and in the United States whom I visited, listened to, and before whom I presented my own understanding of my Nigerian or African culture, as many of their responses helped me in my interpretation of some of the issues confronted in the multiculturalism of the West.

Yet, I must name names here, however few; people very close to me, whose support have meant a lot to me over the yeras: Rahmat Olohuntoyin Na'Allah (Alhaja Karama) and our children, Saarah Haleemah, Rabiah, and Rasheedah; Milan V. Dimić (d. 2007) and his wife, Marguerite Garstin (d. 2007), George Lang, Stephen Slemon, Erica Reckhamp, Abdul-Razak Abdullahi Eleyinla, AbdulHameed Dare Abdul, Abubakar Aliagan, Habibat Malik, and Muhammad Niyi Kamal. At the University of Alberta, Canada, personnel, friends and colleagues of the International Center with whom I was actively engaged in various local and international programming including the Bridge's Program throughout my stay in Edmonton. At Western Illinois University, Fran Hailine, and every one of my faculty colleagues has been of tremendous support!

Chapter 1

INTRODUCTION
꒰꒱

As the pluralism of New World societies continues to grow in the twenty-first century, and the concept of the world as a "global village" continues to form, scholars must, of necessity, study and explan the various cultures of the world to help people know how to better relate to each other throughout the world. Yet, the common phenomenon of our global century, especially from some Western academia, is to interpret non-Western cultures from Western parameters and to apply concepts such as multiculturalism to African societies from Western perspectives, often causing more confusion than clarity and greater analytical problems than solutions.

This is where this book pitches to its theoretical catcher. It is crucial that other societies be explained in simpler terms and easy-to-follow expressions. However, it is useful when we reflect our contemporary world culturally that such discussions are enriched in pluralistic metaphors or multilingual and multicultural codes of the noncybersocieties of cosmopolitan English or French. Such metaphors and codes are not on their own automatic cause for difficulty in language. They are simply symbols of cultural identity in their linguistic diversity. Perhaps the use of the word *cosmopolitan* here presents a challenge that must quickly be surmounted. Cosmopolitan cultures are as well and alive in both traditional and contemporary Africa as they are in the West. Large communities such as Ibadan, Kano, Addis Ababa, and Harare are cosmopolitan in their own right, with cross-cultural family structures and complex social systems from different ethnic nationalities and cultural groups. Yet, the cosmopolitanism of cybersocieties differs in the ways in which electronic technology has greatly influenced daily performance of life and thus affected the ways in which individuals comport themselves, including how their cosmopolitan communities are defined (the term noncybersocieties does not mean a complete absence of cyberspace or cybersurfing). There is also a global cosmopolitanism based strictly on cyberaccess in which, isolated and detached in one's homes or cyberrooms, people daily reach out to all corners of the globe, forming friendships, organizing marital relationships, purchasing goods, or seeking other interests. The global cosmopolitanism (as different from local cosmopolitanism in cosmopolitan Ibadan, Nigeria or Chicago, USA) is rich and variable; yet, it is an antithesis to active orality in ways, for example, that the African marketplace interactions serve as an important agent of socialization and community involvement. Global cosmopolitanism also depends on regular electricity, and on investment in computers, satellites, and, in many cases, other image transmitting softwares and more, which are largely still unavailable to the African village.

We need new works that represent the ideas of those I describe here as active oral cultures in comparison to the passive orality (I have adopted the use of the word "orality" here as a unique reference to state instead of simply "oral." See Ong) of the contemporary West. This book discusses the inherent cultural plurality of the traditional Yoruba and compares it to multicultural concepts of New World societies. It examines Yoruba (and a few other African) concepts of identity, similarity, plurality, and diversity and the different Western concepts of multiculturalism, using Canada and United States as examples. With the migration, exile, and global movement of people from the south to the north into

2

the twenty-first century: it is important to understand what meaning is accorded the new cultural globalization and plurality caused by such movements. For example, what is the difference between the plurality that the Yoruba person represents at home in the Yoruba communities of West Africa before he migrated to the contemporary West and what his or her multiculturalism portends in 21st Century Europe or North America?

The inherent diversity of Yoruba oral culture equips it with a very strong capacity to absorb new cultural forms without causing tension to community's intrinsic structure and identity, whereas the New World communities of the twentieth and the twenty-first centuries depend on government legislation to create and sustain global plurality and multicultural life and identity. In other words, while people of different ethnic groups often attain their multiculturality in "open market" traditions – the African market advertisement and bargaining traditions, the oral griot traditions, the traditions of professional performances by farmers, hunters, blacksmiths, and other oral agencies—in the multiculturality of the written-society people depend most often on formal institutions and on writing. To argue this thesis, I present Yoruba origin stories, explore various kinds of Yoruba oral performances, and later use Ilorin Yoruba identity as a case in point of my discussions.

Yet, as a Yoruba and Hausa speaker now living my plurality in the West, thanks to government legislations in Canada and The United States allowing for residency for foreign students and alien workers, I do not have the same attachment to English as I have for Yoruba and Hausa, possibly because I began speaking English only during my elementary schooling. I started to communicate meaningfully in the English language during my sixth year of elementary school, and to me the English language has been a "sweet burden," and still a burden even if sweet, throughout my postelementary and tertiary education. Though I enjoy speaking the English language, it does not come naturally to me in any way, and, even now, I am always conscious that I am speaking in a foreign tongue whenever I use it. Rather than working to bring my English to the level of an American native speaker,[1] I have found myself forcing English to adapt to my own cultural and linguistic backgrounds.

There may be two possible reasons for any immigrant to a cosmopolitan America to live this similar experience. The first is that the immigrant may not have acquired the English culture with the English language when he or she began to learn English, and so the stronger cultures in his or her consciousness (and unconsciousness) automatically play a role whenever he or she speaks English. This situation resembles what Lado's Mother Tonge transfer theory (1957) poses regarding language learning, where elements in the first language become a Trojan horse in a person's second language learning. The second reason is that the immigrant may have lived for decades in active orality societies such as those of Hausa or Fulani villages or smaller cities in Nigeria and may have been accustomed to being involved in the marketplace, the village center, the town meetings, the naming ceremonies, wedding and burial ceremonies, the blacksmith's shop, the yearly cultural festivals and had listened most of the time to folktales, folksongs of the hunters and the farmers, and their ritual dramatic performances. He likely observed, listened to, and actively participated in an Elaloro (*ela l'oro*) discourse performance in which verbal rhetoric is coated in rich robes of bodily colorations. This person was already a player in the juicy rhetoric of the Hausa and had likely even seen many Hausa cultural forms, performed them numerous times, and understood them inside out. This immigrant has already formed all these lifetime memories. He (or she – any reference to a male here is generic and refers to both gender respectively) is a tree shaped when he was young and has dried under the sun of age. Any effort to reshape him would only break him. And so what is his new global age America going to do for him, the immigrant? Is it going to keep him in his Hausa robes even if in less than perfect English, or is it going to break him into pieces of dried sticks?

My position in this analysis is that I am myself a metaphor for persons who, having lived in active orality societies of the world, feel forced in the twenty-first century to use high-tech languages such as English for reasons of survival and social acceptance. Perhaps if the indigenous cultures of such immigrants had not been active orality cultures like mine was, and if, unlike me, they had grown up in contemporary, largely passive orality societies similar to those in cosmopolitan England, the United States, and Canada, their attitudes to and cultural involvement with English would have been different. In other words, they might have "aligned" with English whenever they spoke English and not brought their Yoruba or Hausa to bear on their English.

Since the trans atlantic slave trade is centuries away and Africans brought to the Americas have become natives to their American homes, is the situation of the black people who speak Ebonics similar to that of a person like me? Do they bring another culture to bear on Standard American English? Can the situation of an oral culture of Nigeria and the "written" or "oral" culture of America's black neighborhood be the same, and can both cultures produce similar responses? In my opinion, the one answer to both questions is yes. I witness that many black people in 21st Century America live in an active orality subsociety—the black neighborhood (see Abrahams 1970; Jackson 1974); and that they largely bring the oral experiences of their up-bringing as background to speaking Standard American English. I am not equating the active orality of the black neighborhood with that of the contemporary Yoruba, yet it is clear that many African American children do not have the opportunity to attend standard and well-equipped schools, and that a notable percentage of those who do have to drop out of school because of the disadvantages inherent in being black in the still largely white United States. I would not be surprised if, like the black ghettos in apartheid South Africa, there are some black neighborhoods in the America of 2009 without schools. Frederick Douglass's (1995: 40-55) experiences while trying to acquire writing and reading skills

5

may still be similar to what some African Americans go through in contemporary America in their efforts to acquire a Western education despite the specious No Child Left Behind slogan of the Bush administration. In other words, although it would not be wrong to say that many African Americans can only boast of oral cultural background from the ghettos, their experiences as far as their exposure to the rights and privileges of cybernetic traditions of the world's most technologically advanced nation is less than desired.

How do I define an active orality society as opposed to a passive orality one? An active orality society is one that exists wherever writing is non-existent. Where writing does exist, it only serves a tiny minority of the population, who, from most indications, do not contribute significantly to the sociocultural life of the majority. The issue of the active orality status is not solely determined by the economic well-being of the population, as a population that is rich and self-sufficient may choose to have little to do with writing. In any case, more often than not, the majority of active orality societies in contemporary Africa live in economic poverty, although they are extremely rich in culture and language.

As I have argued somewhere else,[2] the concept of writing is not foreign to Yoruba or to many ethnic groups in Nigeria. The Yoruba people have many traditional inscriptive signs, e.g., the Ifa script, that are considered writing symbols and are still being used to encode thoughts. However, the traditional Yoruba writing system is very limited and is explored mainly during religious practices such as the *Ifa* divination. The traditional writing symbol called Ge'ez used for Tigrinya and Amharic in Eritrea and Ethiopia for example, is much more advanced, and it plays an important role in local literacy and literary development.

The oral form is the active form of communication for people in an active orality society in which the traditional laws and norms are considered, composed, and conveyed orally. The major form of education among the majority of this populace is informal and oral, and the mass of the community express most of their belief system orally for their daily socioeconomic life activities and rituals such as weddings, naming, burial, inheritance, worship, household governance, and trade. Although the Yoruba today, like the Igbo, Ijo, Ibibio, Hausa, and many other language groups in Nigeria, have a long history of contact with Western literacy, and in some cases even with the Arabic writing system, most people in these language groups are not literate nor do they see themselves ever using writing for anything.

Conversly, in the passive orality societies of the New World, like those in cosmopolitan United States and Canada, virtually everything depends on writing, when we consider the ever-increasing dependency on electronics, writing becomes even more crucial, as computer systems are almost entirely vitalized through writing codes. The new evolution of computer technology in which oral speech fed into computer-generated writing codes, as well as the vocal forms of radio, television, and even the telephone, are forms that depend on huge economic investment, the kind that is practically unattainable by the majority of the population of an active orality society (and this does not undermine my earlier assertion that active orality society is not constructed upon the economic well-being of its population). Electronic forms (even Radio and Television) are built upon writing in one form or another, and basic literacy skills are necessary to operate them. Both Ong and Zumthor have tried in the last century to give their own classifications of societies based on those societies' oral involvement. Ong (1982), for example, identifies what he calls a primary orality society and a secondary orality society and seems to suggest a tertiary orality society as the technological society. However, I have a problem with Ong's idea that primary orality status where no one is influenced by writing is unattainable and therefore nonexistent. Perhaps Ong was talking about the orality society of the North American Indigenous Peoples, and about that of the blacks in America.

Writing systems have penetrated many spheres of Nigerian and Yoruba lives, and elementary schools can be found even in some very remote areas of Nigeria. Yet I insist that there are still many generations of Nigerians whose lives are never touched by writing, just as there are still thousands of languages in Africa, many of them in Nigeria, that have never been written down and have no basic orthography. However, my definition of the active and passive orality statuses, as the terms imply, does not refer either to a total absence or presence of writing form, but rather to the degree of a community's engagement with each of these two systems. The largest population of Yoruba people that live in Nigeria and West Africa even in the global century have few writing skills and cannot read the kind of literature that earned Wole Soyinka the Nobel Prize in literature in 1986. Perhaps 70 percent of the entire Yoruba population can neither read nor write literature of any kind. Conversely, in the contemporary West, although many people may have a low level of literacy education, it is impossible to say that the majority of Western people can neither read nor write!

The scholar of African oral traditions who is him- or herself, born and bred in an African oral community is clearly qualified to assert his knowledge and experiences to enrich his discussion of African orality. The politics of autobiography in the Western world cannot be extended to belittle the right of the African scholar to explore life in theory of culture. He or she, having lived the oral life, is qualified to be a primary source, an interpreter, and a translator of the oral materials of his or her oral culture. In writing this book I indeed assert and claim such rights as an oral and a written scholar of global century plurality. When such a researcher discusses his or her home culture, he or she is discussing his or her own life experiences. This is no less authentic than the confidence contemporary African writers of novels, drama, and poetry have in discussing their cultures in their creative work, e.g., as Wole Soyinka does regarding a Yoruba kingdom in *Death and the King's Horseman* (1975) and as Chinua Achebe does regarding the Igbo world in *Things Fall Apart* (1958). Kwame Anthony Appiah, in his seminal text *In My Father's House* (1992), says he is partially performing his own life in his book, citing profusely from his own past and contemporary family experiences. His argument for a deracialized pan-Africanism in his book, he says, derives from the life he himself saw his father live:

> My Father is my model for the possibility of a Pan-Africanism without racism, both in Africa and in its diaspora—a concrete possibility whose conceptual implications this book is partially to explore. (p. ix)

Despite such cogent arguments by many African scholars, including Appiah, about the level of Westernization of Africa and Africans, I have heard assertions about how much of African identity, e.g., Yoruba, Hausa, etc., has changed because of colonization, and how Africans can no longer claim their original oral culture, let alone resume the position as an expert of it. One of Kwame Appiah's comments is pertinent in rejecting such claims as one of the evidences of the global century ignorance about colonial—past and present—African realities:

> If we read Soyinka's own *Ake*, a childhood autobiography of an upbringing in prewar colonial Nigeria—or the more explicitly fictionalized narratives of his countrymen, Chinua Achebe—we shall be powerfully informed of the ways in which even those children who were extracted from the traditional culture of their parents and grandparents and thrust into the colonial school were never fully enmeshed in a primary experience of their own traditions. The same clear sense shines through the romanticizing haze of Camara Laye's *L'Enfant noir*. To insist in these circumstances on the alienation of (Western-) educated colonials, on their incapacity to appreciate and value their own traditions, is to risk mistaking both the power of this primary experience and the vigour of many forms of cultural resistance to colonialism. A sense that the colonizers overrate the extent of their cultural penetration is consistent

> with anger or hatred or longing for freedom, but
> it does not entail the failures of self-confidence
> that lead to alienation. (p. 7)

European colonization never changed the principal oral reality of much of Africa, including the Yoruba culture of Nigeria. In many villages and towns, a large percentage of children still do not attend the Western-style schools and thus have no access to Western-style formal education (there is, of course, a claim in some quarters that the Yoruba nations combined have a literacy rate of about 50 percent). The rural Yoruba areas especially (without excluding the urban ones) continue to flourish in the oral tradition that Appiah describes as "our own cognitive and moral traditions: in religion, in such social occasions as the funeral, in our experience of music, in our practice of the dance, and, of course, in the intimacy of family life" (pp. 7-8). And this is so even if one is a Muslim or Christian,[3] I myself spent more than thirty years of my life in different types of African communities: in urban, semi urban, and highly rural areas of Nigeria and different from the Africans that Appiah described as "(Western-) educated colonials" (p. 7), I consider myself an African oral cultured person, and I enjoy the "inherent pluricultural" reality of all the oral traditions of my upbringing.

There is no doubt about the significance of the facebook and twit cultures (in actuality it is more facebook than twitter but twitter is also developing fast) that have greatly developed in Lagos and Abuja and many urban cities in Nigeria, where it seems now that about 20% of literate Nigerians that can be described as active global citizens are creating a massive tradition of facebook community, publishing minute to minute diaries of their daily lives and making friends and acquaintances across the world. Mostly postsecondary school students and graduates, National Youth Corps members, and more, go to cybercafés across the cities and on college campuses and spend hours daily on facebook. Nigerian politicians, especially Presidential candidates in the 2011 national elections (notably Goodluck Jonathan, Atiku

Abubakar, and Abubakar Bukola Saraki as early as preparations for primaries) are already active users of this forum to reach these groups of Nigerian elites, but also reach the Nigerian news media as many Nigerian newspapers now source for news directly from entries by politicians addressed to their facebook friends. This is definitely an example of a growing global cosmopolitanism in Nigeria. Vibrant as this may be, the population of primary participants is small due to the fact of the need of certain economic resources to access Internet. The opportunity of a 100 naira per hour cybercafé now readily available in many urban cities in Nigeria has lessened this difficulty for the individual.

Also the increasingly easier and cheaper option to add internet service to cell phone networks provides enormous potential to ensuring faster democratization of cybertechnology for Nigerians such that even in remote villages (especially when there are more solar-powered cheap computers and cell phones), people interested in facebook and twitter can easily post their diaries, tweet, add photos and invite new friends from among Nigerians and others globally as is already popular among literate Nigerians in urban Nigeria.

Finally, the remaining chapters of this book discuss various issues of cultural globalization and plurality from the contemporary Africa of the Yoruba to those of migrants in the New World of Canada and the United States. Chapter 2 gives a general overview of the history, culture, and oral performances of the Yoruba, which is necessary in order to establish from the beginning Yoruba history, identity, and cultural practices and, to relate how most Yoruba people see themselves in their oral culture. Chapter 3 discusses the inherent cultural plurality among the Yoruba and critically compares it with the contemporary pluralism of New World society. My intention in this chapter is to show the differences between cultural plurality in the Yoruba oral culture and the concept of multiculturalism in the global written world. Chapter 4 explains the history and culture of Yoruba Ilorin. The main objective of this chapter is to show how materials from an active orality culture such as Ilorin portray a particular identity of the community.

Chapter 5 foregrounds the points of inherent cultural plurality in an active orality society made in previous chapters, relating them to sociopolitical events in Nigeria. Specifically this chapter argues that many contemporary Yoruba elite, despite their cultural upbringing, failed to allow cultural ethics taught through Yoruba folktales, for example, to reflect on their attitude towards their fellow Yorubas and towards other Nigerians. Chapter 6 returns to the discussion of cultural globalization and plurality in the New World in a way that carries this issue further to the challenges pluralism faces in the twenty-first century. The chapter compares the practice of pluralism and multiculturalism in New World countries, with the process and forms of multiculturalism in the African orality communities. In the New World countries, Native Americans were joined by the Europeans most of whom left Europe either in protest for religious freedom or for colonial expedition, the Africans who were brought as slaves, and later the East Indians, the Chinese and others who were (and still are) mainly economic immigrants. The Whites, mainly Anglo-Saxon, created mainly white cultural domination in most of North America, and also in many areas of Southern America. Contemporary New World countries governments, through congressional or parliamentary legislation, have created political definitions for their own form of pluralism and multiculturalism as pluralism of the faces of immigrants and not of their languages. This has remained what I called the thrust of the New World's cultural pluralism. This is contrary to pluralism in African orality community where pluralism and multiculturalism are left to the "forces of nature" in the open market where there are lesser or no roles for modern African governments or parliamentary legislations. In most cases in Canada and the United States, immigrants are "encouraged" to give up their native languages and identities for the dominant Anglo-Saxon linguistic and cultural traits. This chapter looks at what the contemporary plurality of the West might mean in later years and decades of the 21st Century. Chapter 7 examines the different interpretations people have given to difference, especially racial difference, and how, through travel and cultural reaching-out, personal expectations may lead to inaccurate judgments and thus causing disappointments. The chapter discusses travel, exile, migration, our new pluralistic world and how some people will search and have always searched for cultural acceptance both in their new homes and in their purported native communities. This chapter presents examples from a white physician traveler to Malawi (southeast Africa), an African traveler to Grenada (West Indies), and a Chinese diasporan traveler visiting China for the first time.

Chapter 8, is a response to Henry Louis Gates (Jr.), challenging his interpretation of racial, ethnic, and social differences in Africa in his *Wonders of the African World* video series. The author reexamines what he regards as fundamental errors in the discussion of slavery and servitude of pre-colonial Africa and in the ways that contemporary scholars err in understanding African and New World cultural and social dynamics and how these scholars have brought the baggage of New World racial tensions to their interpretations of cultural and social lives in Africa. Chapter 9 presents an African Islamic cultural performance genre, *Waka*, which has attained important social, spiritual, and popular status among the multicultural Ilorin people of Nigeria.

In concluding this book, I project into the future a continued formation of global pluralism in the West defined only by the faces of immigrants (due to an increasing migration of people from South to North and the continued influence of Western corporations), and I estimate the increasing influence of the electronic superhighway and its twenty-four hour broadcast into Africa. This book predicts the possibility that the "new global century immigrants" defined by the sheer power of population (power of number!) that would force a change in the concept of Western pluralism due to the immigrants' continued attachment to their home and cultural origin, their increased political and economic power in the new countries, and their constant stretch to retain access to their native culture, retain their indigenous languages, and remain regularly involved at their native homes to the extent enhanced by affordable transportation and/or electronic access; thus, causing a real change in the form of plurality of the West. The mere emergence of Barack Hussain Obama first as a 2008 presidential candidate of one of the two major political parties in the United States (and later as the elected US President) is enough reason to accept that the concept of cultural plurality in the West is going through a change because of immigration. The son of a Kenyan father and a white Kansan mother, with the massive support of immigrant communities, young Americans, and a significant percentage of white populations, claims a right to the American presidency. Perhaps one of the most significance of this is that in his campaign, Obama says it is okay to be American and at the same time to learn to speak languages of other parts of the world. This is an idea that the ultra-conservatives seem to think is incompatible with being American. Even though it is far from being revolutionary (and many may not even notice the importance of Obama's stand on the immigration debate during the primary and the postprimary campaigns), CNN's Lou Dobbs and his like-minded friends have already signaled that Obama's proposal for Americans to learn foreign languages constituted a very dangerous push against "one-language plurality" concept in America!

Chapter 2

YORUBA: THE PEOPLE, CULTURE, AND ORAL PERFORMANCES

"When Elephant dances in a forest, the spirits of the forest, the trees, the birds who fly around singing in sonorous voices and provide juicy music to the dance already know who the Elephant is!" I heard similar words sung so melodiously to me in Yoruba by an Ilorin freelance poet just before I left home for overseas in 1994. He sang that the birds' voices wouldn't be as titillating, that the dance would be awkward, and that the Elephant would miss his steps if those who compose his music, however melodious their music sounded, did not invoke his lineage names. Elephant, *Erin* in Yoruba, is a praise name of his patron, *Erin jogun ola*, "Elephant inherits royal vibrancy!"

My preoccupation in this chapter is like that of the birds in the Elephant's forest. I cannot enhance the dancing steps of my Yoruba cultural plurality theory without showing how well my songs know Yoruba's praise names. This chapter must spell out the background of the meaning, origin, and cultural structure of Yoruba, so that when its Elephant dances, all visitor audiences and members of the household would not need a soothsayer to interpret its steps. Says one

Yoruba adage: "When we acknowledge seeing an Elephant, we know that we have indeed seen an Elephant, as the mighty animal cannot be described as 'a tiny tail that flipped by'" (*Taa balaari erin, aama pe ari erin, ajanaku kuro ni mori iru kan firi*). Through several available written sources, oral stories, and performances in prose and poetry, this chapter intends to establish the historical origin of the Yoruba nation and offer background information about its inherent cultural plurality. I show how, despite colonization and contemporary neocolonial cultural influences in Nigeria, the Yoruba culture retains its identity and, through its continued vitality, helps the Yoruba people, regardless of the differences among them, to define their Yorubaness.

As far back as 1980, when writing his famous book, *The Yoruba Today*, J. S. Eades confessed to the following:

> Writing a general book about the Yoruba is a foolhardy enterprise, a fact which is clearer to me now than when I began it. There are two main problems. The first is the sheer mass of material available: the Baldwins' bibliography (1976) has nearly 3500 references, to which I could add a few hundred more. (P. ix)

As I am writing almost three decades after Eades made this statement, it would be an impossible task to cover in this little work all that has been said and written about the Yoruba to date. Yoruba people are in my view, a sophisticated language group in Africa, and not just because a Yoruba writer (Soyinka) exploring the language and mythology of his people was the first African to win the Nobel Prize in literature but also because Yoruba has drawn such a wide range and high amount of attention from researchers around the world. A work such as mine can only mention or, at best, rush through a few of the things that have been researched to date about the history and development of the Yoruba people. In this chapter I invoke a Yoruba discourse strategy, *Elaloro*, and further develop the argument about the inherent cultural plurality of the Yoruba. My intention in discussing

Yoruba historical origin, Yoruba culture, and oral performances in this chapter is to add more stars to the clear sky of the evidences of Yoruba inherent cultural plurality. I do not merely narrate the history or culture of the Yoruba here but use such materials in critical polemics.

Just as Chinua Achebe said about the Igbo, *Yoruba* was not a universal concept; neither was it a general identity of all the Yoruba language speakers until sometime before European colonization. However, unlike the Igbo, it did not take a civil war to create a "powerful consciousness" (Appiah 1992: 177) of Yoruba identity among the speakers, although—as I have mentioned earlier—the family, the village, and the language subgroups (otherwise called speakers of different Yoruba dialects) continue to be important references to the people. It is interesting to consider the way five different authors discuss how the name *Yoruba* came about:

1. The country was probably first known to Europe from the North, through the explorers of Northern and Central Africa, for in old records the Hausa and Fulani names are used for the country and its capital; thus we see in *Webster's Gazetteer* "Yoruba," West Africa, East of Dahomey, area 70, 000 sq. miles, population two millions, capital Katunga. These are the Hausa terms for Yoruba and for Oyo. (Johnson 1921: xix)

2. The term Yoruba is sometimes said to have been derived from a foreign nickname, meaning cunning, given to the subjects of the Alaafin of Oyo by the Fulani and Hausa. The Hausa word for Yoruba is *Yarbanci*. Yoruba has been commonly applied to a large group, united more by language than by culture, whose members speak of themselves as Oyo, Egba, Ijebu, Ife, Ilesha and the other names of the various tribes. (Forde 1951: 1)

3. [As] these various groups of people were known in Sierra Leone only under the name Aku, the label, Yoruba, as that of an ethnic group could not have been long in vogue prior to 1856. It is indeed possible that, before being used to refer to the whole people, this name first gained currency only after the journey of Captain Clapperton from Badagry on the Gulf of Guinea to Katunga (Old Oyo or Eyeo). In the account of the journey published in 1882, he referred to the whole territory through which he passed on that journey as the country of the Yarriba and to the people themselves as the Yarribans. This name he adopted from the Hausa, who applied it, apparently, to the people grouped together as Yoruba who were nearest to their own territory, that is the Oyo-Yoruba kingdom. (Fadipe 1970: 29-30)

4. Until recent times the Yorubas did not consider themselves a single people, but rather as citizens of Oyo, Benin, Yagba and other cities, regions or kingdoms. Oyo regarded Lagos and Owo, for example, as foreign principalities, and the Yoruba kingdoms warred not only against the Dahomeans but against each other. The name Yoruba was applied to all these linguistically and culturally related peoples by their northern neighbors, the Hausas. (Courlander 1973: 2)

5. Indeed, the use of the word "Yoruba" to refer to the whole area is surprisingly recent, dating only from the middle of the 19th century when it was introduced by missionaries and linguists (Law 1977:5). It is derived from the Hausa word for the Oyo Yoruba, and they are still sometimes called the 'Yoruba proper' to distinguish them from the other major subgroups. Yoruba-speaking groups in the Benin and Togo republics refer to themselves as "Ife" rather than as "Yoruba" (Igba and Yai 1973). (Eades 1980: 2-4)

It is fascinating to note that a word coined by the Hausas for *Oyo Yoruba* became the name the speakers of the language use to describe themselves and their community. This development shows how, in active orality, one culture can easily nativize or indigenize names, concepts, and cultural practices from or used by another. For example, why was it that Bariba, another oral culture and language group, had such an influence on the Yoruba as to have contributed to the way Oranmiyan, a Yoruba forefather, chose the settlement later called the ancient Oyo? According to the oral tradition reported by Samuel Johnson, the king of Bariba directed Oranyan to use a particular charm in locating a new settlement:

> Tradition has it, that the king of Ibariba made a charm and fixed it on a boa constriction [sic] and advised Oranyan to follow the track of the boa and wherever it remained for 7 days and then disappeared, there he was to build a town. Oranyan and his army followed his directions and went after the boa up to the foot of a hill called AJAKA where the reptile remained for 7 days, and then disappeared. According to instructions Oranyan halted there, and built a town called OYOAJAKA. This was the ancient city of Oyo marked in ancient maps as Eyeo or Katunga (the later being the Hausa term for Oyo) capital of Yarriba. (Johnson, p. 11)

The interaction among individuals and ethnic groups in oral culture goes beyond the surface level as each treat the other as human beings first rather than as Yoruba or Hausa or Bariba, easily accepting each other's tradition and way of life as authentic and human. For Oranyan to have accepted the charm from a Bariba king shows the respect and trust each ethnic group had for the other. Although they might be meeting for the first time, both groups demonstrated that a human being not be a "stranger" in the other's company. In Yoruba history, it was not only the Hausa or Bariba that benefited the Yoruba; the Yoruba language also has many enviable records in the histories of many other neighboring language groups. Ethnic groups have occasions of disagreement and conflicts between one another, examples of which we mention later in this chapter. However, it remains important that such conflicts were not based on the consideration that one was more "human" than the other, or that one culture was intruding on the other (which seems always to be the bases for discrimination in New World societies).

To come back to the issue of the name *Yoruba*, I have no quarrel with the possibility that this word originally meant "cunning" (Forde, p. 1), or that it perhaps comes from the word *wayo*, as cunning individuals are called *mai wayo* in Hausa. However, it is more likely, as has also been argued, that the original name, *Yarbanci* or *Yarriba*, comes from a Hausa word *raba*, "divide" or from the sentence *Ya raba*, "he/she divided [it]" (see Forde, p. 1; Fadipe, p. 30). In my opinion, there is also a possibility of another word, *riba*, meaning "gain" or "profit," which Hausa itself most likely borrows from Arabic. After all, *riba* may be easily established as the root word for *Yarriba*. Whatever word the name *Yoruba* comes from, it is clear that it has a connection to the open market orality culture and likely derived from trade or transactions. *Cunning, divide, gain* or *profit* are words people use in a traditional market.

The way the Yoruba name came about further confirms my contention that Yoruba active orality is not hostile to cultural influences, even though such influences might have to go through a process of nativization. Otherwise, the Yoruba would not have accepted a name from a sister ethnic group. Many words and concepts in Hausa can also be traced to the Yoruba language, as to all the other languages that have active oral contact with Hausa. However, such an analysis does not fall within the scope of this work.

The Yoruba-speaking people occupy an area, described by Eades as the "Yoruba homeland" (p. 1) and by N. A. Fadipe as "Yorubaland" (p. 21), in southwestern Nigeria, as outlined by two writers:

1. South Western Nigeria, from the Guinea Coast west to the Niger Delta, 200 miles inland to the Nigeria where it flows south-west to join the Benue, and extending west into Dahomey and French Togoland. The most westernly groups are on the right bank of Mono, to the north and south of Atakpamé. (Forde, p. 1)

2. The Yoruba country lies to the immediate West of the River Niger (below the confluence) and South of the Quorra (i.e., the Western branch of the same River above the confluence), having Dahomey on the West, and the Bight of Benin to the South. It is roughly speaking between latitude 6° and 9° North, and longitude 2° 30' and 6° 30' East. (Johnson, p. xix)

Within Nigeria alone, Yoruba language, one of the many in the country, and Yoruba people have several dialects or subgroups: Oyo, Egba, Ife, Ijesa, Ijebu, Ondo, Ketu, Ilorin, Ekiti, Yagba, Akoko, Owe. Among important sources on these different ethnic groups are Daryll Forde's *The Yoruba-Speaking Peoples* (1951) and Samuel Johnson's *The History of the Yorubas* (1921). The British colonization of Yorubaland introduced some specific political dimensions to the life of the Yoruba people, as it did to all the other ethnic groups in Nigeria. According to J.S. Eades (1980: 5):

> [T]he colonial powers imposed their own administrative structure which has undergone several modifications. Nigeria was initially divided into provinces which were subdivided into divisions and districts. In addition to the Lagos Colony, four provinces in Southern Nigeria had predominantly Yoruba population: Abeokuta, Ijebu, Ondo and Oyo. In Northern Nigeria there were substantial Yoruba-speaking populations in Ilorin and Kabba Provinces. In 1934, Oyo Province was split up, and Ibadan Province was created.

21

There have been several interesting developments since Nigerian independence from the British, especially after the Nigerian Civil War (1966-70). Many more states were created in Nigeria, the latest being in 1996 with the redivision of Nigeria into thirty-six states. As of 2008, however, the Yoruba people in Nigeria spread across seven of the Nigerian states: Lagos, Ogun, Ondo, Oyo, Osun, Ekiti, and Kwara. Some people would like to add Edo to the list of the Nigerian states where Yoruba is spoken, and this is debatable.

The Yoruba can also be found in the neighboring West African countries of Benin, Togo, and Sierra Leone. In the Americas, descendants of Yoruba slaves can be found in Cuba and many other Caribbean islands. Yoruba are known by different names such as *Aku* (Sierra Leone), *Ana* (Togo), *Anago* (Dahomey), and *Lakumi* (Cuba). Various other names are used among some Yoruba subgroups in Nigeria (see Eades 1980: 1-3).

The Yoruba language belongs to the Kwa language group of the Nilo-Saharan subfamily or the Sudanic language family (Fadipe 1970: 55) and shares the same subfamily with some Nigerian languages, i.e., Igbo, Ebira, Nupe, Ibibio, Edo, among others (see Eades, p. 4). Among the most important features of the Yoruba language is the tone. Tone is as important to Yoruba as stress is to English. It accounts for changes of meaning in Yoruba words. For example, in midtone sounds, ókó, means "husband"; midhigh tones, *Ókò* means "vehicle or machine"; and the tone can be slightly changed again to mean, "hoe." Fadipe has more good examples on Yoruba tone and also discusses Yoruba syllables and vocabularies in his textbook *The Sociology* (1970) (see p. 55).

Yoruba vocabularies come from many root words, borrowed words, and sometime words and concepts nativized from many neighboring languages. Some words were adopted from the colonial language, English, and are used mostly among the urban Yoruba. The most important of Yoruba words include names of persons and their bodily parts, names of nonhuman beings, names of concepts, abstract and concrete; and words indicating parts of speech such as verbs, adjectives, adverbs, and prepositions. Yoruba forms its phrases by compounding and by the use of adjectives, adverbs, and other parts of speech. Many new words are also formed through compounding, duplication, and reduplication as well as through affixation and derivations. It can be easily said that Yoruba people always find it easy to create new words in the language. Airplane: *ero ayara bi asa*, meaning literally "machine [that is] as fast as the hawk." The word *ero* denotes something that is being smithed or fabricated; *riro* is "the act of creating or smithing." The word for radio is *asoro ma gbesi*, "that which speaks without waiting for response." Some new words are formed through adoption and modification. For example, university is *fasiti* and professor is *kofeso*. I must, however, emphasize that some of these words, especially the adopted ones, can only have meaning among urban Yoruba or the elite who can read and write. With the numerical or numeration system, Yoruba developed a cowry currency that no doubt helped them to create a system of oral numerals, and thus, according to Fadipe,

> [T]he Yoruba have a well-developed system of numeration. There are three different and parallel classes of numerals which, though formed of the same root words, are, nevertheless, distinguished one from the other by the definiteness of the mechanism by which they are formed. (p. 61)

Later on in this chapter I discuss sociopolitical activities among the Yoruba, especially such activities as marriage and kinship to which oral forms are central.

On the origin of the Yoruba people, two important theories still survive. How or from where have the researchers obtained these theories? Samuel Johnson explains how they came to us from oral sources:

> The National Historians are certain families retained by the King at Oyo whose office is hereditary, [they] also act as the King's bards, drummers, and cymbalists; it is on them we

depend as far as possible for any reliable information we now possess. (P. 3)

The first origin story is about how the Yoruba came from Mecca to their present place, and here I will reproduce N.A. Fadipe's summary of the relevant part of the tale:

> [T]he Yoruba came from Mecca to their present abode, having been driven out of Mecca following a civil war between Oduduwa and his followers who were conservative and did their best to enforce a return to idolatry and the Muslim party. Oduduwa died before he could organise an avenging expedition against the party which drove him out of his native land. It was left to his grandson Oranyan to do this, his own son Okanbi having died before him after Oduduwa's death. The expedition did not proceed very far, however, before it broke up owing to dissension between Oranyan and his brothers. Out of shame Oranyan would not return to Ile-Ife from which he had set out, but settled down on or near the site of Old Oyo (called Katanga in Hausa) which subsequently became his capital. He had left his treasures and fetishes in Ile-Ife in charge of a trusted servant, Adimu, who was also charged with carrying out the worship of the national *òrìsà* (godlings). This servant was given undisputed authority in Ile-Ife after he himself had settled down in Old Oyo. Thereafter, whenever he needed anything from among these treasures, he sent word to the servant. ... through thus performing some of the most important duties of a king, namely, the religious functions, Adimu was practically raised to a kingly status. (Pp. 33-4; also see Johnson, pp. 3-14)

The second Yoruba creation myth is rather long but may lose its special mythical touch if I simply summarize it. The story postulates that the Yoruba were created by *Oranyan*, otherwise called *Oranmiyan*, at the beginning of time. I reproduce most of this creation story below, and I hope the reader, while imagining that he or she is listening to an oral narration of this Yoruba creation myth, will allow his or her inner voice to read aloud to him or her and will perhaps feel the mythical effect that a typical Yoruba listener feels when such stories are narrated:

> In ancient days, at the beginning of time, there was no solid land here where people now dwell. There was only outer space and the sky, and far below, an endless stretch of water and wild marshes. Supreme in the domain of the sky was the orisha, or god, called Olorun, also known as Olodumare and designated by many praise names. Also living in that place were numerous other orishas, each having attributes of his own, but none of whom had knowledge or powers equal to those of Olorun. Among them was Orunmila, also called Ifa, the eldest son of Olorun. To this orisha Olorun had given the power to read the future, to understand the secret of existence and to divine the process of fate. There was the orisha Obatala, King of the White Cloth, whom Olorun trusted as though he also were a son. There was the orisha Eshu, whose character was neither good nor bad. He was compounded out of the elements of chance and accident, and his nature was unpredictability. He understood the principles of speech and language, and because of this gift he was Olorun's linguist. These and the other orishas living in the domain of the sky acknowledged Olorun as the owner of everything and as the highest authority in all matters. Also living there was Agemo, the Chameleon, who served Olorun as a trusted servant.
> Down below, it was the female deity Olokun who ruled over the vast expanses of water and wild marshes, a gray region with no living things in it, either creatures of the bush of vegetation. This is the way it was, Olorun's living sky above and Olokun's domain of water below. Neither

kingdom troubled the other. They were separate and apart. The orishas of the sky lived on, hardly noticing what lay below them.

All except Obatala, King of the White Cloth. He alone looked down on the domain of Olokun and pondered it, saying to himself, "Everything down there is a great wet monotony. It does not have the mark of any inspiration or living thing." And at last he went to Olorun and said, "The place ruled by Olokun is nothing but sea, marsh and mist. If there were solid land in that domain, fields and forests, hills and valleys, surely it could be populated by orishas and other living things."

Olorun answered, "Yes, it would be a good thing to cover the water with land. But it is an ambitious enterprise. Who is to do the work? And how should it be done?"

Obatala said, "I will undertake it. I will do whatever is required."

He left Olorun and went to the house of Orunmila, who understood the secrets of existence, and said to him, "Your father has instructed me to go down below and make land where now there is nothing but marsh and sea, so that living beings will have a place to build their own towns and grow their crops. You, Orunmila, who can divine the meanings of all things, instruct me further. How may this work be begun?"

Orunmila brought out his divinity tray and cast sixteen palm nuts on it. He read their meanings by the way they fell. He gathered them up and cast again, again reading their meanings. And when he had cast many times he added meanings to meanings and said, "These are the things you must do: Descend to the watery wastes on a chain of gold, taking with you a snail shell full of sand, a white hen to disperse the sand, a black cat to be your companion, and a palm nut. That is what the divining figures tell us."

Obatala went next to the goldsmith and asked for a chain of gold long enough to reach from the sky to the surface of the water.

The goldsmith asked, "Is there enough gold in the sky to make such a chain?"

Obatala answered, "Yes, begin your work. I will gather the gold." Departing from the forge of the goldsmith, Obatala went then to Orunmila, Eshu and the other orishas, asking each of them for gold. They gave him whatever they had. Some gave gold dust, some gave rings, bracelets or pendants. Obatala collected gold from everywhere and took it to the goldsmith.

The goldsmith said, "More gold is needed."

So Obatala continued seeking gold, and after that he again returned to the goldsmith, saying, "Here is more metal for your chain."

The goldsmith said, "Still more is needed."

Obatala said, "There is no more gold in the sky."

The goldsmith said, "The chain will not reach to the water."

Obatala answered, "Nevertheless, make the chain. We shall see."

The goldsmith went to work. When the chain was finished he took it to Obatala. Obatala said, "It must have a hook at the end."

"There is no gold remaining," the goldsmith said.

Obatala replied, "Take some of the links and melt them down."

The goldsmith removed some of the links, and out of them he fashioned a hook for the chain. It was finished. He took the chain to Obatala.

Obatala said, "Now I am ready." He fastened the hook on the edge of the sky and lowered the chain. Orunmila gave him the things that were needed--a snail shell of sand, a white hen, a black cat, and a palm nut. Then Obatala gripped the chain with his hands and feet and began the descent. The chain was very long. When he had

27

descended only half its length Obatala saw that he was leaving the realm of light and entering the region of grayness. A time came when he heard the wash of the waves and felt the damp mists rising from Olokun's domain. He reached the end of the golden chain, but he was not yet at the bottom, and he clung there, thinking, "If I let go I will fall into the sea."

While he remained at the chain's end thinking such things, he heard Orunmila's voice from above, saying, "The sand."

So Obatala took the snail shell from the knapsack at his side and poured out the sand.

Again he heard Orunmila call to him, saying this time, "The hen."

Obatala dropped the hen where he had poured the sand. The hen began at once to scratch at the sand and scatter it in all directions. Wherever the sand was scattered it became dry land. Because it was scattered unevenly the sand formed hills and valleys. When this was accomplished, Obatala let go of the chain and came down and walked on the solid earth that had been created. The land extended in all directions, but still it was barren of life.

Obatala named the place where he had come down Ife. He built a house there. He planted his palm nut and a palm tree sprang out of the earth. It matured and dropped its palm seeds. More palm trees came into being. Thus there was vegetation at Ife. Obatala lived on, with only his black cat as a companion. (Courlander, pp. 15-19)

It appears to me that Harold Courlander, in relating this story, simply translates the wording of the oral narrators, following their pauses and inserting their high and low tones. This story had been narrated to me many times as a child, and even though the areas linking the parenthood of the *òrìsà* to *Olorún* seem a little strange to me, the narrative clearly brings alive one of the Yoruba's important theories about the creation of the world. Does this kindle in the reader the type of mystical feeling the story rekindles in me? That is one of the purposes of providing the lengthy quotation above: to offer the reader the kind of experience a Yoruba child derives from listening repeatedly to legendary and mythical stories such as this creation myth. Imagine a young child, from about three years of age, in the most moving oral narration possible, being introduced to the concept of multiple gods (as many as five Yoruba deities have already been mentioned in the above story), diverse beliefs and worships, and the idea of plurality within his own "small" language, cultural, and spiritual worlds! To make the long story short, *Olorun* later sent *Agemo*, the chameleon, to the earth through the golden chain, where he found that the place was a huge space of darkness. Because of Agemo's report, *Olorun* made the sun, which gives light and warmth. But, according to this story, Obatala soon discovered again that despite the company of his cat, he was lonely, and so he "decided to create people" (Courlander, p. 19). Using clay from the ground, he molded human shapes and dried them under the sun. After an exhausting job, he resorted to drinking the inner liquid of the palm trees, and, being drunk from the wine, he continued shaping his objects; but this time, under the influence of the wine, he made many very crooked shapes. Thereafter, he consulted *Olorun*, saying, "I have made human beings to live with me here in Ife, but only you can give them the breath of life" (quoted in Courlander, p. 20). Olorun answered his call by putting life into the shapes, and thus they became the first people on Earth, people of various shapes, some normal and others physically challenged, like cripples, etc. This story further narrates how the creatures began to worship the various deities, i.e., *Obatala, Olorun, Orunmila, Olokun,* and *Esu* (see Courlander, pp. 21-3).

The Yoruba are the most urbanized African precolonial people, with the cities of Ife, Oyo, Ibadan, Abeokuta, Ijebu-Ode, Ilesa, and Akure as a few examples of urban Yoruba cities. For a long time, Ibadan was said to be the biggest city in West Africa. In many ways, the Yoruba society has not changed very much despite contemporary influences on the

Nigerian society. Except for the elites who, due to new riches and material acquisitions resulting from the post-independence oil boom (see Apter 1996: 441-66), build houses and live outside the traditional family compounds, most Yoruba in semiurban and rural areas continue to live largely in *agbole*, the "family compound," with their parents, grandparents, uncles, children, and grandchildren—sometimes up to four or five generations of family members, often with the oldest male member as the *bale*, or "head." Membership at the *agbole*, however, is not always limited, either by oral tradition or contemporary reality, to blood relatives. What Daryll Forde said as long ago as 1951 about the Yoruba *agbole* remains true in 2009:

> The men of the component families need not, however, be members of a single patrilineage ... two or more of these may be represented. In Ife it is regarded asconsisting of three distinct sets of people; the *omole* (*omo ile*: descendants of the house) the members of the patrikin (*ibatan*) which established the house or compound; the wives of male members of the *omole* and finally "strangers" in the compound, i.e., other men admitted as residents, but not assimilated to the "owning" patrikin and who may be patrikin among themselves, together with their wives. The term *omole*, however, includes daughters even when they have left the co-resident group at marriage. Such resident daughters of an *omole* are also referred to as *omo osho*. (Forde, p. 11)

The Yoruba people define a Yoruba community as *kaaro oojiire*, wherever people traditionally speak the language now called Yoruba. *Kaaro* (or *Eku owuro o*), means, "Good morning" and *Oojiire* means "Hope you woke up well (or Did you wake up well?)" It is a phatic communion among the people, and traditional ethics require people to ask after each other and to enquire about each other's health. The Yoruba are one of the African ethnic groups that have a very extended form of greeting, a different one for a different purpose, such as when one is seen standing, sitting, eating, sleeping, in the morning, afternoon, evening, during the raining season, the dry season, harvest, droughts, etc., and ethics demand that a properly cultured Yoruba know when and what greeting form to use at each of these times. It is little wonder then that the simple way the Yoruba community is defined is *Ile Ekaaro, Oojiire*, "the land/community [where people say] good morning, hope you wake up well."

One important feature of Yoruba speech is the use of respect pronouns. Social and age hierarchies are very important, and respect pronouns are common words of very precise usage. A traditional ruler is respected, whether or not he is an elder by age, since rulership in most communities is by inheritance rather than age. Sometimes age can play a role in choosing a successor. In any case, the king or chief is most likely not the oldest person in the community. He is, however, regarded as the eldest since he is also seen as representing the ancestors and having the authority of the gods. The Yoruba say, *Oba, ekeji orisa*, meaning "King, deputy to the *orisa* deity." In Oyo, it is *Alaafin ekeji orisa, iku babayeye* which may mean "Alaafin, deputy of the deity, the death of fathers and mothers.") Indeed there are many other seniority levels that do not depend on age, like the seniority of wives in a compound or at the first family level. Also, in the larger community, issues such as family size, hard work, money and material wealth, or spiritual position are used to determine status (see Forde, p. 11).

A person of subordinate status does not address his elder by name but uses respect pronouns instead. For example, a younger brother directly addresses his elder one as *egbon*, and while speaking to him or her uses the second person, *eyin*, or the third person, *awon*. Both *eyin*, and *awon* serve also as plural nouns (their singular forms are *iwo, ohun*, i.e., "you", "him" or "her"), but in this case they are respect pronouns. Therefore, translating literally, when a younger person is directly addressing or talking about his elder brother, he says, using *eyin* or *awon*:

(A).

1. *Mo n ba eyin soro* (*Mo n baayin soro*) - I am talking to you (English does not have a clear equivalent of *eyin*, which is the respect word adopted in this position by the Yoruba, but "you" in the translation of Yoruba sentence to English language is the type one would use for two or more people, like using the French *vous* for a singular subject).

2. *Awon* - They (the respect pronoun, meaning, however, his elder brother or sister) are coming.

3. *Ti awon ni iwe yi* (*Tiwon ni iwe yi*) - This book is for them (respect pronoun, "them," meaning only one person, his elder brother or sister).

The pronoun does not change when the elders being addressed are two or more, in which case it will serve as both plural and respect marker.

When, however, an elder is addressing a younger person he or she says, using *iwo* "you"; or *ohun*, "him" or "her":

(B).

1. *Mo n ba iwo soro* (*Mo n bao soro*) I am talking to you (singular, no respect pronoun).

2. *Ohun n bo wa si ile* (*O n bo wa sile*) - He (or she) is coming home.

3. *Ohun lo ni iwe yi* - This book is for him (or her).

However, in a situation where the younger one is in a higher social or traditional status like the king, queen, or traditional chief, the elder brother addresses him or her as in (A) above. It is believed that the younger person who occupies the position of *agbalagba* (an elder) is him/ herself an *agbalagba*. In other words, eldership is not attained solely by age. The Yoruba do not take kindly to disrespectful behavior. They consider it as a sign of pride and pomposity, which may attract some punishment in the form of verbal rebuke or alienation. For example, a child who introduces his father's elder or younger brother to a stranger as "My father's brother" is assumed by this "father's brother" to be saying that he (the uncle) has no responsibility or authority over him (the child) and thus is not of importance to him (the child). This is a terrible insult in family circles, and the "father's brother" may react by either rebuking him or by withdrawing whatever support he gives him as required by the local custom, which is usually the same as the one that the person's biological father may give to him. The child is expected to address his uncle as "Father," *Awon baba mi (baami) ni ki e yoju sawon*, literally meaning, "My father needs your attention (or asks that you come over to see him)," and the child may be delivering this very message to his own biological father from his uncle.

As we can see from previous usage, Yoruba pronouns do not have gender distinction, and words such as *ohun*, *awon* (third person), *iwo*, and *eyin* (second person) do not indicate gender. Also, in Yoruba family relationships, concepts such as uncle, aunt, niece, nephew are not in common usage. In fact, there are no Yoruba words for them, and the speaker must formulate the concept using phrases or sentences. It is considered rude for a child to introduce his father's brother as an uncle instead of a father, as noted above, or his mother's sister as an aunt instead of a mother. Also, both of these people introduce him as their son (or daughter in the case of a female). There is no such word as "cousin," as every person is an elder, *egbon*, or a younger one, *aburo* (both *egbon* and *aburo* are gender neutral).

There are no people richer than the Yoruba in oral performances, though all the oral cultures in Nigeria are indeed very rich. The Yoruba people love merrymaking to the extent that virtually every occasion for it includes a kind of oral performance. The Yoruba sing and dance at birth, at marriage, and at death. During all these events oral singers are engaged to entertain the people. Forms of oral performances are limitless among the Yoruba. Apart from the ones that

33

are well known across the culture, there are many oral genres among subgroups. Persons interested in Yoruba oral forms will discover new forms every day; the farther they travel, the more they will see. Ulli Beier, in classifying genres of Yoruba oral poetry, recognizes *Oriki, Ese ifa, Ijala, Iwi, Ekun Iyawo*, and *Alo apamo* (see "Yoruba Poetry," p. 20). However, Babalola (1964: 20) adds *Rara, Ofo, Ogede*, and *Iyere Ifa* (also Ruth Finnegan 1970: 79).

According to Olaitan Olatunji (1970: 8), Yoruba oral poetry is classified not by its themes but by the styles in which it is rendered and by its contents. Olatunji classifies Yoruba poetry into two categories, i.e., "chanting modes" and "content types" (p. 9). Those poems he calls chanting modes are the ones recognized by their chanting styles. *Rara, Ijala, Asa, Ekun Iyawo* and *Iyere Ifa*. Babalola (1966) and Olajubu (1972; 1980) write very extensively on *Ijala* and *Iwi* respectively. Most of these forms are explored in contemporary compositions such as *Apala, Sakara, Waka, Fuji,* and *Juju*. One genre specific to Yoruba language subgroups includes, *Orin Opa* in Kabba Bunu. In Ilorin there are *Dadakuada, Ere Baalu, Kakaki, Ere Olomooba, Were, Waka, Orin Makondoro,* and *Toobeni* (see Na'Allah 1987: p. 6; p. 9).

In addition to oral poetry, many Yoruba also enjoy community-based festivals and ritual performances. Most of the time the festivals and rituals include poetry, dance, and mime, and costume and involve a larger community of people, young and old. In some annual festivals, like the *Awon* festival in Saho (see Na'Allah 1997b: 125-42), the community comes together to marry young women off to eligible suitors. Similar festivals take place among the Ogori Magongo people of Nigeria (see Na'Allah 1994a: 112-15). There are Yam Festivals, which usher in yam harvests and the eating of new yams in many Nigerian Yoruba and non-Yoruba communities in Nigeria. Some festivals are dedicated to deities such as *Sango, Oya, Osun, Ogun, Obatala,* and these events can be found in many Yoruba communities. Plenty of food and drink is provided during festivals, as people are generally very generous. What these festivals have provided for the Yoruba are special occasions—be they births, weddings, or deaths—where the people can always explore oral performance, dance, listen to music, sing, mime, and participate in other things that the festivals offer.

I would like to explore another example regarding written culture and its interaction with oral culture in Nigeria. The result, of course, differs from what one may get when one oral culture interacts with another oral culture and shows how an active orality society can coexist with a written culture within its own territory. Islam and Christianity among the Yoruba are the best examples of written culture in an active oral environment, and this assertion does not in any way diminish the importance of orality in these religions, especially in Islam, in which the oral form is crucial (see Graham 1987).

We do not appease lions in order to pretend that elephants are insignificant to the peace of the forest. To discuss contemporary Yoruba without calling on the elephants of the modern Yoruba culture would be grossly incomplete. Islam and Christianity are also so deeply ingrained in the Yoruba culture that sometimes it seems that these two religions, as some Yoruba people practice them, are inherently Yoruba. After all, some arguments do link both religions to Yoruba (see Johnson, pp. 3-11). As long as seven centuries ago, there was evidence of a strong Muslim population among the Yoruba, including both the peasantry and the royalty. Evidence of this continues to show, for even in the house of Oyo Yoruba the Islamic religion has been well rooted. The current Alaafin of Oyo, Abdul-Hameed Adeyemi, is a Muslim, as was his father (also formerly an Alaafin). Yoruba communities such as Iseyin, Saki, Ibadan, Kisi, Osogbo, Ilorin, and Lagos have a significantly high population of Muslims. It was only two centuries ago, around 1823, that Christian Missionary Society (CMS) came to Badagry and started, with later missionary groups, missionary work that took them all around Yorubaland and many other areas of Nigeria. Abeokuta, Ife, Ilesa, Ijebu, Ondo are among Yoruba communities with very large Christian populations up to the twenty-first century. It may be erroneous to insist that one of the two religions has the greater following among the Yoruba, since no census has been done to determine the figures.

One of the implications of the involvement of Islam and Christianity in an active orality community is the fact that since both religions have written scriptures (their tenets clearly stated in writing), they have to contend with the reality of orality in Yoruba culture. (I discussed parts of this issue in a paper, "Orality as Scripture: Verses and Supplications in Yoruba Religion") Today, among some Yoruba Muslims and Christians, traditional Yoruba oral forms have come to complement their written scriptures in worship and in their proselytization methods.[1] In Ilorin, for example, some Islamic preachers have adopted traditional oral forms, reaching out to Islamic adherents and sometimes delivering songs alongside Qur'anic verses during public preaching. The following is an example of such songs, called *Orin Esin*, but its performance mode was originally taken from *Rara*:

> *La ilaha*:
> ko s'Oba meji nibikan
> *ila'llahu*: af'olohun.
> Ohun ni n seje, Ohun ni n semu
> N ningbo bukata aawa eda
> eda o mookan wale aye
> eda o ni mookan rorun
> iwa teda ba wu ni teda
> ise teda ba see ni teda
> iwa teda bawu ni teda
> al-humma an-nabi ejare
> kaman ja s'orun lofifo. (Na'Allah 1989: 20)

> *La ilaha*:
> There is no two gods anywhere,
> *Ila'llahu*: except Allah the Almighty.
> He provides food, He provides drinks
> He answers all people's callings
> A human creature brings nothing to the world
> A human creature shall take nothing to heaven
> The character displayed by a person is his (only)
> possession

The good deeds of a person are his (only) possession,
Umma of Annabi, males and females of you,
Human being must endeavor to strive hard (in
doing good)
So that he doesn't go to heaven in emptiness.

Another Muslim song, similar to *Ewi*, has also been performed by a Muslim preacher:

Olowo aye won o nisimi
Olola aye won o nisimi
talaka aye won o nisimi
kinni o je olowo aye le ni simi?
ki n mamaku, kowo o mama tan
ko je kolowo aye lee ni simi
kini o je olola aye le ni simi?
ki n mamaku, ki won o ma yo mi
b'oba ba bimi, kini n o fo fun
ko je kolola aye lee nisimi
kini o je talaka aye o le nisimi?
ki n un o maje, kini un o ma mu
bi lamayin tito ni un o ma to
ko je ki talaka aye lee nisimi. (See Na'Allah 1989:
19-25.)

The rich of the world have no rest
The royal of the world have no rest
The poor of the world have no rest
What denies the rich of the world rest?
"Oh, I don't want to die, I don't want my riches
to perish,"
Would never allow the rich of the world to rest
What denies the royalty of the world rest?
"Oh, I don't want to die, I don't want to be deposed
If the government asks me, what explanation
shall I give?"
Would never allow the royalties of the world to rest
What denies the poor of this world rest?
"What shall I eat, what shall I drink?
What that person achieved I want to achieve"
Would never allow the poor of the world rest.

The above *Ewi*-like song is characteristically philosophical. It adopts repetition, question, and direct speech techniques to discuss what it calls "restlessness of human beings" in the world. The involvement of oral performances in Islamic activities among the Yoruba is so strong that some Yoruba Muslims employ Yoruba singers to sing for them (some singers, freelance, just go to sing whether or not they are invited) when they return to Ilorin from the holy pilgrimage to Mecca. In one such instance, I recorded the following song:

> Oba Oluwa lawa mama ki
> La mama ki, Oba Oluwa lawa mama ki
> Al-hamdulillahi
> Adupe lowo Oba eda oo
> Alabi re maka o mama bo
> oju wa t'awon ota oo
> Oba Oluwa, Oba Oluwa lawa mama ki.
> (Alabi Ramani, Apala artist, Field Performance, Alore, Ilorin, 20 May 1990; see Na'Allah 1994b.)

> It is God Almighty that we praise
> He is the One that we praise, it is God Almighty that we praise
> Alhamdu li llahi (thanks be to Allah)
> We expressed our gratitude unto the Creator of mankind
> Alabi went to Mecca and returned safely
> And the enemies are shamed
> Certainly it is God Almighty, it is God Almighty that we praise.

The above song alleges that the celebrant has an enemy who would have been delighted if he had died during the pilgrimage. According to the singer/oral poet, it is only God, and not human beings, who should be praised for ensuring the successful return of the celebrant from Mecca. In many ways such a belief by the oral poet is derived from traditional Yoruba culture just as the praising of "the only One God" is derived from Islam.

Poetic rendition is a principal part of Christian religious rites in Nigeria. There are quite a number of hymn books compiled for Christian worship in and outside of churches. However, my research reveals that traditional African songs and performances have found their way into Christian religious hymns and songs. Some churches even allow traditional *Ewi* and *Ijala* (see discussion of Yoruba oral forms in chapter 3) poets to come to church and chant praises for the bride and the bridegroom during wedding ceremonies. The following examples are traditional Yoruba songs that have been incorporated into Christian hymns:

> E ba min ra baba ko Oba ogo o
> Oba a terere kaari aye
> oti terere deele mi o
> Oba a terere kaari aye.
> (Church Services, C & S Church, Sabo-Oke,
> Ilorin, 24 February 1991; see Na'Allah 1994b)

> Do please come en-mass to greet the benevolent
> God
> The God-who-spreads-everywhere-in-the-world
> He is present in my house
> TheGod-who-spreads-everywhere-in-the-world.

The song is rendered during church services amidst dancing and clapping. God is described as *Aterere kaari aye,* one "who-is-everywhere-in-the-world" or "who-spreads-everywhere-in-the-world." This is how the Yoruba describe the *Olodumare,* the Supreme Being. It seems then that the above song was adopted from Yoruba praise poetry. One Yoruba elder, Alabi Omolabi, age eighty-five, reproduced for me what he claimed came deep from the Yoruba's traditional praise poetry:

> Oba mi,
> ariwa riwa
> arinu r'ode
> aroju r'eyin
> a terere kaari aye.

(Alabi Omolabi, Agbarere, Ilorin, 27 February
1991; see Na'Allah 1994b)

My God,
He who-sees-the-past, who-sees-the-future
He who-sees-the-inside (mind), who-sees-the-
outside
He who-sees-the-front, who-sees-the-back
He who-spreads-all-over-the-world.

There are several arguments by scholars on whether Olodumare is regarded as omnipresent and omniscient in the Yoruba
worldview (see Gbadegesin 1991: 87-93). It is clear, however,
from the above songs that the Yoruba see Him as capable
of being everywhere and as being supreme in His authority.
However, this may also be a result of the indigenization of
Islamic and Christian concepts, which is now causing arguments and counter arguments among contemporary scholars. Segun Gbadegesin has well summarized such arguments
in his discussion of "Traditional African Religiosity: Myth
or Reality" (see pp. 83-104).

Incantation and magic have also been incorporated into
some Christian forms of worship in Nigeria, just as they
have not been jettisoned by some Muslims in their daily
lives. Evidence abounds on Christian pastors and bishops
employing incantations in their verbal deliverances. One of
my sources alleged that many pastors use magic and meta-
physics to lure people into attending their churches. We also
confirmed, through discussions with some Yoruba people,
that many Yoruba Muslim preachers and Christian pastors
wear traditional Yoruba magical strings, *onde*, around their
waists, usually to command respect and signify authority
among the people in places of worship. This development,
which some adherents of Islam and Christianity claim is a
sin against God, is certainly what Lanrewaju Adepoju, an
Ibadan chief and a recently avowed Muslim crusader, refers
to in his *Ewi* poetry:

Irun ni gbogbo wa n ki nile Oluwa ...

awa o ma ye eeyan totunfi onde s'ibadi wa si
Masalasi,
bo ba je pe won n'igbago ododo, emi ni gbere tun
nse loju won?
Eeyan kankan o si ni mu dudu ma Oba yaarabi
ki'le aye e o toro
oruka Ogun tee fi sowo ni soosi nko, kilode o
igbagbo tee ni seleda o to ko?
Ese bi boya Oluwa lee ntan je ni ...
(Lanrewaju Adepoju, "Oro Oluwa" LALPS 142,
1990; see also Na'Allah 1994b)

It is prayer we all observe in the house of God
We do not know the number of people who put
magic strings around their waists to the mosque
If they do have honest belief (in Allah), what does
incision want on their faces?
No person will ever combine evil with God
Almighty and still have a successful life, What
about the Ogun ring that you put on your finger
in the church?
Is the belief you have in the Creator not enough?
You think it is God that you deceive ...

My research shows that the forces of traditional oral culture
are penetrating deep into Islam and Christianity practices
in Africa, regardless of such condemnations from preachers like Lanrewaju Adepoju. In fact, there are churches in
Africa today, called "African churches," that try to promote
African culture and to synthesize it with traditional Christian churches practices.

The most astounding evidence of the influence of
African active orality on modern "written" religions (Islam
and Christianity) is the infiltration of *ofo*, magical incantations, into the sermons of some Yoruba pastors, bishops,
and Muslim mallams. In one instance, at the beginning of a
Sunday service, a pastor chanted the following:

Omin ni n poro ina
ojo gbiriri ni n pa oro ogbele

gbogbo awon ota wa
ki ina maa jo won.
(Personal interview with A.A. Joseph, 26 February 1991)

It is the water that kills the poison of fire
It is the thundering rain that kills the dryness of
the land
All our enemies, let the fire burn them.

Water, the archetypal representation of purity, peace, and godliness, is at war with fire, the archetypal representation of evil and destruction. The pastor concerned is invoking power of water against fire, the symbol of the evil of his enemies. He also commands fire to destroy all of his and his congregation's enemies. It is possible that the pastor, like the *babalawo*, the *Ifa* priest or the oracle man, or like an African magician, has an alligator pepper in his mouth or even an *ase*, a magical incision on his tongue. He certainly does not use incantations only for aesthetic effect. Also, while welcoming someone who was reverting to Islam, the imam, a Muslim leader of salat prayer, offered many prayers and recited from the Holy Qur'an and added the following chants to reassure those who feared that the person could be harmed by enemies:

Eyi ti n je eni ba deeru leeru n to
gbogbo eni to ba pe ti e laburu
aburu ni o ma je tie na.
(Adeyi Compound, Ilorin, 17 February 1991)

Which means that whoever blows ashes into the
air will have ashes coming after him;
Whoever talks ill of you
Will have ill for himself.

Ashes are seen as an element of destruction, and blowing ashes at or on a person is seen as a wish for that person's destruction. The above incantation is meant to provide a full sense of security for the person the performer is facing.

In any case, it is clear that in active orality, it is not easy to hinder the influence of oral culture. It is a living force within society. Although the impact of Western education has not yet threatened active orality, in this chapter we discussed further how Yoruba culture continues to prosper despite the importation of American television culture.

Indeed, no culture is static. Every culture is dynamic and thus changes according to developments within and around it. It would be strange, even wrong, to say that Yoruba culture, or any culture subject to the massive Western influence the Yoruba have gone through, will not change in any way. History and contemporary research show that Yoruba culture has consistently undergone such changes, but these changes are not enough to support the hypothesis that the Yoruba, or better put, the Egba, the Ilorin, the Ijebu, the Oyo, etc., have lost their identity. Social and cultural activities among the Yoruba in 1998 show that as a predominantly oral society, Yoruba society has not lost its ability to indigenize and nativize the foreign elements with which it comes into contact with its ability to represent them in its own local form. It makes such forms a part of its own culture rather than maintaining them as English, Hausa, Fulani, Igbo, or Arabic.

A good example is how the urban or city Yoruba have responded to the influx of the video and television culture of the 1990s. Rather than allowing these Western mediums to continue to project Anglo-American and foreign cultures in Nigeria, they adopted them to suit the local tastes and use them for films featuring local cultural realities. They embark on massive oral cultural productions on radio, television, and video and recent research confirms that in 1996 in Nigeria more films were released in local languages than in English (see Schmidt 1998: 2). Filmmakers realize that most of Nigeria is still an active orality society and that to reach the greater part of people they must produce films appealing to that oral society even for urban centers. Producers such as Ogunde (deceased), Jimoh Aliu, Lateef Adejumo, Ola Adeyemi, Adegboyega, Moses Olaiya, Yemi Eleburuibon, and others made and continue to make films and video documentaries on oral performances.

Yet oral poetry and festivals, oral performances, and radios and television and films are not the only way for the Yoruba to enjoy their orature. Very early in the morning, when a child gets up from bed, his grantparents chant his praise names; each time he does something good for the elders in the compound, they remind him of his ancestry through songs and tell him about how brave and courageous and good his great grand parents were. The mother has lullabies with which she lulls her crying baby to sleep. The kids have games, such as hide and seek, pure songs, and some involving acting and role-imitation. The marketplace is another fertile area of Yoruba oral performance. There are advertisement songs *orin ipolowo oja* almost everywhere in the locality. There are free-lance poets around the market singing to whomever cares to listen and appreciate their songs. Musical accompaniment is crucial in many Yoruba songs. The *Iyaalu, gangan, omele, agogo, dundun, sakara, akuba, bembe* are a few of the drum types used to provide beautiful music to Yoruba songs. Both the drummers and the singers are called *ayan*, as we mentioned as an example in the first chapter. Being an *ayan* is a serious business. In some families it is hereditary. The Yoruba have some oral performers who perform in obedience for the gods. For example, the *Ologun ijala* beggars perform strictly on the command of the *ifa* priest. Another *ijala* performer, the trained *ijala* artist, performs on occasions such as weddings and naming ceremonies.

The telling of folktale is also a very interesting example of performance that involves every member of the household. It is always an opportunity for parents, grandparents, and elders and younger children to come together and participate in folktale sessions. Folktale sessions are one of the instances when the elders are able to interact on an affectionate level with their children and the children are able to be close to their grandparents. The elders give them moral education through folktales, and they create opportunities for the children to learn to sing, dance, and even make mistakes in the narration of the tale, thus preparing them for much bigger performances at village centers or community festivals.

This chapter has established that the Yoruba are an inherently diverse group. In fact, it shows that the concept of plurality is rooted in its very origin. The Yoruba creation story promotes the concept of the plurality of gods, goddesses, deities, and worships. Also, we have discussed that the Yoruba, because of the active use of oral performances and traditions among them, continue to be an active orality society. This chapter also demonstrates the sustenance of plurality features in oral performances and other sociocultural practices among the Yoruba. Islam and Christianity, as examples of written cultures in contemporary Yoruba society, depend heavily on Yoruba oral forms for proselytizing. Despite the influences of written cultures such as contemporary Western culture or Islam and Christianity, the Yoruba people have always found ways to remain loyal to their cultural identity.

Chapter 3

THE YORUBA INHERENT CULTURAL PLURALITY

Elaloro! This book does not need to sacrifice to *Olukoso* (Sango, a Yoruba deity), as my literary hunter will not compete for an antelope in its forest. If I vie at all for a prey, my only weapon in this book is *elaloro*, rhetoric resonating in dialogue, songs, and stories, and I pay homage to *Oloogun Ijala*, the singing lord of the hunting forest. The previous chapter showed that Yoruba culture, despite colonization and the vigorous contemporary importation of Western pop culture through electronic media into Nigeria, retains its identity. Their traditional culture continues to help the Yoruba define their Yorubaness. This chapter therefore discusses the Yoruba's intrinsic cultural plurality in contrast to Western concepts of multiculturalism.

Notwithstanding the large number of ethnic groups in Nigeria, the Yoruba, just like any active orality culture, continues to thrive adequately within multiple ethno-cultural spaces. Indeed, from our discussions in chapter 2, it is clear that the idea of plurality is not new to traditional Yoruba culture, as Yoruba culture is intrinsically pluralistic. For example, the Yoruba people have a plural concept of god and goddess, and of religious beliefs. Any Yoruba believer in Yoruba deity is free to worship any or all of the gods as he wishes or to whichever god the *Ifa* directs him.

Some of the important points in the two Yoruba origin stories narrated in chapter 2 strongly support a theory of the inherent cultural plurality of the Yoruba:

1. The Arabia origin and the move from Mecca to the present place indicate the possibility of meeting several ethnic and cultural groups on the way and being influenced by such groups; one example is the Bariba group.
2. Reverend Samuel Johnson's rejection of the Arabia/ Mecca link and his argument of possible connection between Yoruba Coptic Christian, Nimrod, or Upper Egypt.[1]
3. The issue of religion or worship that can be traced to the origin of the Yoruba; oral tradition shows that they began as worshipers of several gods and deities.[2]

Again, these origin stories enable the Yoruba to refrain from being obstinate about what they bring into their religion, culture, or way of life, provided such forms can be nativized or indigenized. Such incorporation does not threaten their sense of Yorubaness, their family solidarity, or their community identity. It is interesting to note that some important Yoruba oral traditions were indigenized from neighboring oral cultures. One important example is the *Egungun* masquerade cult among the Yoruba, I have dedicated a chapter in my book "African Discourse in Islam, Oral Traditions, and Performance" to this Egungun-Yoruba connection. The summary of my submissions is that *Egungun* traditon was originally from Nupe and was therefore intro- duced into Yoruba from that culture.[3] Given the importance of Egungun in Yoruba culture, from its ancestral concept to its spiritual and metaphysical essences as an indigenous reli- gion practiced by the Yoruba, perhaps it would be surprising to many that we have presented strong evidences that locate the origin of Egungun in a non-Yoruba culture.

I have gone this far in discussing the *Egungun* connection in Yoruba culture to show how receptive oral cultures are to other oral cultures. I have shown the kind of conflicts that may arise in an effort to "discriminate" and resist the so-called foreign culture. Like human beings, relationship between cultures must not be treated as a "I" or "we" vs. the "other". It must be accorded a treatment of a "we" and a "we" relationship, as equals in an opportunity for cultural and linguistic interaction and dialogue. Multiculturalism in New World nations (such as Canada and the United States) lacks what I regard as "correct" relationship, and thus lives every day in cultural tensions. An active orality society is more vibrant and more receptive of other cultures; it does not give up its own identity to them, but it "welcomes" them into its house and makes them natives of its country. Contemporary debate in the United States about immigration and the immigrant's language is presented as if the recent immigrant (a legal or illegal one) is inferior to the American who himself is a great-grand child of an immigrant since he is not a Native American. Recently, even the idea that American children learn Spanish and other foreign languages in a global age is treated with disdain in ways that suggest that those immigrants and their languages are not worth being understood by the American. For example, Barack Obama had just won his party's primary, having acquired the number of delegates needed and emerged the presumptive candidcate of his party for the national election. As one of the hottest issues debated during the primary was on the immigration problem and what each candidate proposed to solve it, Obama repeated his idea that while English must remain the only offocial language in the United States, every American child should be open to, even encouraged to, learn and become functional in a foreign language. As far as he was concerned, this would enable the American child to become better equipped for the global market.

Soon enough, an angry Lou Dobbs of the CNN castigated Obama as a politician that has contempt for the American people (July 2008). Dobbs said Obama was suffering from elitism and a lack of understanding of the real struggle of the ordinary American. Dobbs compared this Obama proposal to Obama's California fundraising speech, where the candidate had said Americans in the rural areas clung to guns and religions in the face of hardship economic conditions. He said Obama must apologize to Americans for daring to ask them and their children to learn Spanish or another foreign language! Lou Dobbs representes a view in America that is intolerant of immigrants, seeing them and their languages as subservient to the Americans and American English. I would not be surprised if people of Dobbs's type see British, Australian, and New Zeeland immigrants to the United States, even though already English speaking, as needing to do away with their variations of English for the American one in order to properly become equal to the English speaking American. We discuss this further later in this book (see chapter 4).

The point I am trying to make with this example is that the topic of the Obama-Dobbs debate (if we can call it that) is not tenable in the orality society of Africa where multiculturalism is not legislated upon. It is the drive of the open market and a process of functional social balance that bring about multiculturalism and multilingualism or the learning and acquisition of multiple cultures and languages, and whether a governor or a legislator likes it or not, or a news anchor or a talk-show host hates it or not, people are naturally drawn towards acquiring more languages and becoming multilingual. As they meet other people who speak a different language within only a hundred of kilometer away from their own community, and as speakers of other languages bring good and services to the market during market days, they are presented with an open opportunity to know other people and they grab such opportunity with passion. As a culturally plural society, such a behavior is only natural and even when there is quarrel and misunderstanding among peoples and ethnic nations, acquiring languages of other peoples does not become a matter of hate and ridicule.

One experience that I personally had as a small child is of my maternal grand mother, Halimatu Iya Lele, who had traveled widely as a young person all through market days in near and far away communities from her Ilorin city and who therefore spoke many languages of the northern Nigerian neighborhood. Unfortunately I did not research this before her death, but I am certain it will not be an exaggeration to say that she spoke about 20 languages that are indigenous to the North of Nigeria and other languages spoken in Benin, Niger and Chad. Even at the time I was much too young to fully comprehend, the excitement with which she used those languages whenever itinerant people were passing by or came calling at her home, and how she felt at home with guests, strangers and even those she did not know, demonstrated some quality to her behavior which I am now certain are unique to people who truly live plural cultures and enjoy the advantages of multicultural and multilingual personality. From such a tender age of about 7, I knew I wanted to be like my grand mother, and wanted to have the kind of excitement and passion I saw in her eyes whenever people different from her came around. Much as the American kid of the twenty-first century has an enormous opportunity for an open cultural plurality, it is the kid's parents such as Lou Dobbs that are keeping them locked up in a narrow and myopic corner in which they are constantly afraid and dejected, rather than passionate and excited, whenever they come across people of other cultures and ethnic languages on their streets. The opportunity that comes with America being the destination of many peoples from across the world has not translated into a thinking of cultural plurality for a typical American child. It will never translate to this until the Lou Dobbs of America stopped seeing immigrants to the USA as a threat to Americanism but rather see them as an enriching factor to a healthier and new form of pluri-Americanism: American of multiculturalism and multilingualism, where not only the immigrants' faces matter but also their languages and cultures are important.

The kind of Americanism that caused the State of Arizona in 2010 to promulgate the Arizona immigration law (SB1070) that criminalizes, in my opinion, people's racial and ethnic identities is not the Americanism that can be described as a healthy Americanism. The Arizona immigration law in question invites law enforcement to use racial profiling against people of color, thereby in my opinion, officially promoting acts that betray fear of the immigrant. I really believe that this law has mandated that a person's racial or ethnic look is enough reason to arrest him or her under a suspicion of being an illegal immigrant. This Arizona legislation, a form of "force" that New World society uses to define its own multiculturalism, has caused a lot of tension with the Obama White House. Many observers have described the Arizona law as a direct confrontation with the US Federal Government because immigration is often seen as being within an exclusive Federal jurisdiction. Already other States like Florida is considering similar laws as Arizona. I am afraid this might become the order of the day for mostly conservative governed states in the USA.

Yet in another development, and similarly betraying the fear of the non-white ethnic and linguistic identify, the same State of Arizona has enacted another law, HB 2281, which seeks to ban "ethnic studies programs" in the state's public educational institutions (Randall Amster 2010). In an article, "Arizona Bans Ethnic Studies and, Along With it, Reason and Justice", Randall Amster describes these actions as "ethnocide". Here is Amster:

> While much condemnation has rightly been expressed toward Arizona's anti-immigrant law, SB 1070, a less-reported and potentially more insidious measure is set to take effect on January 1, 2011. This new law, which was passed by the conservative state legislature at the behest of then-school superintendent (and now attorney

general-elect) Tom Horne, is designated as HB 2281 and is colloquially referred to as a measure to ban ethnic studies programs in the state. As with SB 1070, the implications of this law are problematic, wide-ranging, and decidedly hate-filled. Whereas SB 1070 focused primarily on the ostensible control of bodies, HB 2281 is predominantly about controlling minds. In this sense, it is the software counterpart of Arizona's race-based politicking, paired with the hardware embodied in SB 1070's "show us your papers" logic of "attrition through enforcement" that has already resulted in tens of thousands of people leaving the state. With HB 2281, the intention is not so much to expel or harass as it is to inculcate a deep-seated second-class status by denying people the right to explore their own histories and cultures. It is, in effect, about the eradication of ethnic identity among young people in the state's already-floundering school system which now ranks near the bottom in the nation.

(Randall Amster 2010)

There are no better examples than the recent Arizona laws, SB 1070 and HB 2281, that show how New World society's conservatives hope to stop the rate of immigration into their country, and through it, kill the ethnic identity of those who already immigrated, protect the dominance of the English language and the White culture, even as their nation's constitution "promotes" a so-called multicultural society.

Chapter 4

IDENTITY, CULTURAL PLURALISM, AND CULTURAL ACCOMMODATIONS
ᗦᗙ

The question in Nigerian oral cultures, especially in Hausa and Yoruba oral traditions, and I believe in most African oral societies, is never whether there is diversity, or whether there are differences in oracles and oracle worshipping. I should reemphasize that the traditional Yoruba alone have about 401 deities, and there are major differences and similarities in the worshipping of each of them. Among Yoruba language speakers, as among Hausa and many active orality language speakers with which I am familiar, there are many dialects, and in some cases speakers of some dialects barely understand speakers from others even though they are speaking the same language. These are evidence of the cultural plurality of the oral society, and not an indication that the people look for or play on such differences in defining their relationship with each other. For example, oral forms in African oral communities are performance based: oral narratives, poetry, drama, and festivals are communally performed. Just as an Asante great-aunt would call her nephew by the names of her ancestors, a Yoruba would do the same, by giving to her "nephew," from birth, her own great-grand father's name and calling him only by that name for as long as she lives. Like the Asante king, the *Alaafin* (the king of Oyo), among the Oyo Yoruba people, has the *Oyomesi* to guide and advise him in council. The processes of consultation, deliberation, and other oral performances in the palace happen often in Oyo, Zulu, Yoruba, Hausa, and Nupe palaces just as they do in an Asante palace. The people present would use the *Kaabiyesi* formula if they were Oyos in Alaafin's, or Ifes in Ooni's palace; they would prostrate themselves and beg the king to ask for forgiveness for an erring child, just as in the Asante culture. And similarly, the Olórì (*Abusua* in Asante; see Appiah 1992, p. 187) would often join in asking for the forgiveness of the king, more so if she were the child's great-aunt—Not because she is trying to pretend to be in sympathy with the child, but because tradition requires her to do so. If a person goes to the traditional Hausa market, he would see that the Hausa enjoy the same "open spaces" as Yoruba, Tiv, Okrika, Asante, or Kanuri women. And those who know contemporary Yoruba society well enough know that even in the Yoruba's Oyo Alaafin there are women who are in "enclosed horizons" and who are "forever barred from contact with men other than [their] husband[s]" (Appiah 1992, p. 25).

I attempted, in my Introduction to *Ogoni's Agonies*, to define multiculturalism as a multiethnicity of the world, the oral world mixing with the written world in what is now called a "global village." In other words, a multicultural world is like the multicultural United Nations: a comity of nations of the world, each with its own different culture and language, and where differences, rather than similarities, are emphasized. I also related it with the example of a multiculturalism of the English written by many contributors to *Ogoni's Agonies*. I called that multicultural English a language that "breathes Euro-American as well as African cultures" (p. 5). The tension that can be observed between the monocultural and the multicultural users of the English language, one claiming the other user inferior or the other user's English unacceptable, is a good example of the tension in the New World society's multicultural reality.[1]

Nigerian novelists such as Chinua Achebe, Gabriel Okara, and Amos Tutuola, among others, brought their indigenous language idioms into English and perhaps thus created a love-hate situation in the English world. For years, up to the close of the twentieth century, many British and American English speakers would refuse to recognize these African writers' works in the English language as deserving of any literary value. Many departments of English would not even include their writings as samples of literature in English language. The Lou Dobbs of America would even treat white immigrants from Britain, New Zealand, Australia, as inferior English speaking immigrants. They would show unequalled disdain to hear that immigrants from Nigeria, Zambia and Zimbabwe also claim to speak English.

My point is that the nature of multiculturalism in the New World is a love-hate relationship of tension, suspicion, and disrespect. All these negativities are uncommon in the cultural pluralism of an oral society such as that of the Yoruba. This is not to say that there is no conflict in contemporary African communities, but these conflicts have nothing to do with the issue of diversity. Tensions and inter-ethnic wars such as the 1996 genocide in Rwanda or the mistrust in 1998 among the ethnic groups Nigeria or the 2008 ethnic massacres in Darfur, Sudan, are consequences of colonial legacies and contemporary bad leadership in Africa, the neocolonial tragedy of our day. The haphazard colonial arrangement of African communities into dubious nation-states is not meant to function! For years to come the world will continue to witness more near severances of these marriages of inconvenience in Africa. It will be like an art of magic if the results of the future referendum in the Sudan do not lead to the separation between North and South Sudan into two different countries.[2]

It is clear therefore that, using Yoruba oral community as an example, the Western concept of "multiculturality" would not correctly convey the situation in oral Africa (including, especially, contemporary communities outside the urban seats of African neocolonial governments). My point, as I have mentioned above, is that the hundreds of deities and religions among the Yoruba, and the fact that every adherent worships his or her god without friction with worshippers of other gods, shows how active orality exists in a peaceful intrinsic cultural plurality. Also *Ifa* (the Yoruba god of divination), when consulted by its believers, may ask them to sacrifice to or to worship a different god from the one they worship, and that person would do so without hesitation. In other words, the idea of plurality is inherent among the Yoruba people, and it is not strange to them that some people would have a different appearance from theirs or that some ideas would be completely opposed to theirs or that some people would choose to present a pluralistic outlook either in their personality, ideas, worship, any area of human, cultural, and spiritual endeavors. Although the Yoruba are a very proud people and will often insist on having a very sophisticated culture, the Yoruba have an oft-used proverb: *Omo ti ko ba de oko elemiran aso wipe ko si oko to to ti baba ohun*, meaning that "A child who has never been to another person's farm boasts that no other farm is as big as his father's." The point is that with anything sophisticated there is another more sophisticated elsewhere! Although I have heard some Yoruba persons refer to neighboring oral cultures as being inferior to the Yoruba, I have yet to see any doctrine in the Yoruba language and culture that conceives others shabbily because of reasons of cultural or racial difference. I do believe that the pluralistic outlook of the traditional Yoruba accounts for the important successes achieved in the peaceful convertion of Yoruba people to Islam and Christianity and in the often-peaceful relationship that traditional religion adherents have always sought to forge with Christians and Muslims. Most of the religious tention we hear about, in Nigeria at least, is always between Christians and Muslims.

Indeed the Yoruba believe in the concept of the *eleda*, i.e., the creator, in the idea that every person is created according to the wish of the *eleda*, and that it is an insult to the gods, in particular to Obatala, whom Yoruba call the chief architect of human beings, to discriminate against a person because of his physical or biological realities, especially if they are traits he is born with. As Appiah (1992, pp. 3-27; 173-80) clearly argues about the un-Africanness of pan-Africanism, a racial basis for pan-Africanism would sound very uncultural to a traditional Yoruba.

The Yoruba believe that a person's *ori* (head or destiny) determines his importance or lack thereof. There is an adage, *Ayanmo o gboogun, ori eni lawure*, meaning that "What a person becomes does not require magic, one's head is his good fortune medicine." The Yoruba also insist that every person has an *eleda* spirit, and so even when that person is absent he should be treated as if he were present whenever anything concerning him is to be done. The Yoruba believe that *bi enia o si nibe, eleda re wa nibe*, meaning that "if a person is not there, his *eleda* is there."

Other Yoruba concepts, *Omo enia* (human being) and *Aye*, (the world), are not defined by race (Gbadegesin, 27-59). Yoruba believe in the similarity in human attitude, and they see all human beings as capable of both good and bad acts. And *aye* can be both "the world" as an abstract idea or "human beings/people" as both a physical and/or abstract concept. Odolaye Aremu, an Ilorin oral performer, has a very interesting praise poem for *aye*:

> Eniyan soro ema se f'eniyan sere
> N je baa r'eke o a s'ebenire ni (pause)
> Aaye e
> Eru aaye yi le bami pupo ojo
> Omo eeyan ti n gbegi togun laase
> Aaye n binu kanhun, won da kahun s'omi
> Aye n binu iyo, won dayo s'eepe
> Aye n binu Edu ni won ba geka Edu ku kan.
>
> People are difficult, please never take people lightly
> Whenever we see a cunning person, we think he
> is a good person

59

Aayee! This world!
I'm afraid of this world:
The child of a person who cuts the tall tree from
its underneath
When the world is annoyed with *kanhun*, potas-
sium, they pour *kanhun* into water
Whenever the world is annoyed with *iyo*, salt,
they pure iyo on the sand
Whenever the world is annoyed with Edu, they
cut all of Edu's fingers but one.
(qtd. from Na'Allah 1988: 103)

Odolaye's songs clearly show the Yoruba's understanding of a person's capacity to degenerate into a "human beast." Since he can cut off another person's fingers, and probably kill that person, extrinsic or intrinsic racism, as Appiah calls it whether in apartheid South Africa, America, or Nazi Germany (see Appiah 1992, 13-17), cannot take the Yoruba aback; to them human beings have innate tendencies that result in the most pusillanimous acts possible. In other words, the Yoruba do not discriminate against people, even regarding this capacity for evil.

Yet, it will be erroneous for me to say that the Yoruba, because he or she sees humanity as one, has no concept of group identity, e.g., the Yoruba identity, the African iden-tity, or the black identity. The Yoruba believe strongly in family and group solidarity. The individual, as a member of the family or group, shares the collective identity of his lineage and is expected to safeguard the name and image of his family or lineage. A very important Yoruba adage goes, *T'enin teni tekisa ntaatan*, meaning that "What is yours is [importantly] yours, what belongs in the garbage is [can only be] the rags." This adage emphasizes relationships based on family lineage, household, town, or any social group. Every person is expected to watch out for his own group or family member. Although, as I have emphasized before, "race" is not an element of social recognition among the Yoruba, it is, however, difficult to say whether a Yoruba person would not easily recognize race, such as the black as *t'enin teni*; after all, one can argue that people of the same race do have some-

60

thing in common and thus form a group. The Yoruba word that comes close to "race" is *iran*, but it may also mean family lineage, such as when it appears in the Yoruba phrase, *Awon iran baba re*, "Your father's family lineage." Yet race or racism can come out differently in the Yoruba language. The Yoruba rendition of he word or phrace, apartheid or racist government is *Ijoba eleyameya*. In this sense *eya* is used to mean discriminating against a skin color different from one's own. However, in Yoruba *eya* traditionally means something separated out for a purpose, not necessarily negative; although it is now difficult to use the English word *discrimination* for anything positive, it does not in itself always connote negetivity. In Yoruba a person can still say, *o yaa si oto*, or *yiya soto*, meaning "He (or she) keeps it separately, or the process of separating for recognition/difference"; the root word (*ya*) is open to many usages and meanings, especially as its tone changes; alternately meaning drawing, separating, lending, tearing, branching. The proverbial concept that *bi ewe bape lara ose a di ose*, meaning that "if a leaf stays long enough on the body of soap, it becomes soap," is very popular among the Yoruba and is often used by them to show that any person is capable of gaining a group's or family's acceptance, even if he does not originally belong to that group or was not born into that family.

It is important to take another look at Kwame Appiah's assertions on the issue of identity, which seeks to deny racial identity, or any identity at all. For example, it may be largely true that race is an unusual basis for identity formation in many oral societies, including that of the Yoruba; nevertheless, the issue of identity is crucial to the Yoruba's sense of pride and to defining their religious, cultural, and sometimes even economic perspectives. Although they may have only called themselves Oyo, Egba, Ondo in the past rather than Yoruba,[3] it does not reduce their sense of collective identity even in that past. To explain a concept as important as the identity concept among the Yoruba as "an invented history" or as "false presuppositions" (1992: 174) is to seriously miss the point. Even though, as I have already stated, race may not be a yardstick of identity among the Yoruba, just as it is not so among many African cultures, the Yoruba still think that every person deserves an *oruko*, name, which is basically the center of every person's, family's, or community's identity. One adage says, *Oruko rere o san ju wura ati fadaka lo*, meaning that "A person's good name is more important than gold and silver." The family name is seen as a major factor in family identity and so is jealously guarded. Identity is linked to lineage, to ancestors, and to the very being of each family and often includes the political and economic realities of their lives. For example, among the Yoruba, a Blacksmith, Goldsmith, or a hunter has his profession reflected in his family, lineage names, and praise poetry, as does a warrior, ruler, and medicine man/woman or herbalist. In many situations these professions and positions are hereditary, passed from generation to generation. While race may not be central to identity formation among the Yoruba, a Yoruba person is specially empowered by his identity and draws his history and essence from it. Ethnic marks among the Yoruba, as much as they convey beauty and even metaphysical essences, are primarily marks of identity and lineage history. Among the marks cut on Yoruba faces are *keke*, *abaja*, *ondo*, *pele*; and they are all symbols of family and lineage ancestry.

An African identity may be relatively new; after all, the name *Africa*, and its concept as a continent, came about only a few centuries ago. Africans themselves are not new to the idea of exploring the advantage of their collective being or their group identity. The African Union and all other such continental and regional organizations on the continent are certainly modern, but they do not teach concepts of naming and identifying to Africans. I strongly believe that Appiah has misinterpreted Achebe's perception of the Igbo identity. Achebe had said:

> "The duration of awareness, of consciousness of an identity, has really very little to do with how deep it is. You can suddenly become aware of an identity which you have been suffering for a long

time without knowing. For instance, take the
Igbo people. In my area, historically, they did not
see themselves as Igbo. They saw themselves as
people, from this village or that village. In fact in
some place "Igbo" was a word of abuse; they were
the "other" people, down in the bush. And yet,
after the experience of the Biafran War, during
a period of two years, it became a very powerful
consciousness. But it was *real* all the time. They
all spoke the same language, called "Igbo," even
though they were not using that identity in any
way. But the moment came when this identity
became very powerful ... and over a very short
time." (qtd. in Appiah 1992: 177)

As I understand it, Achebe is saying there is nothing "shift-
ing" in the Igbo identity or in their definition of it. As quoted
above, Achebe asserts about the Igbo: "They all spoke the
same language called 'Igbo,' even though they were not using
the identity in any way." Whoever is familiar with Igbo
history knows that they lived in clans, and so the family,
the village, or the clan was the major level of self-definition,
rather than the "nation."

As is evident in my discussion of the Yoruba, even though
they once had a kingdom and a history of living as a nation or
empire, the family lineage or the household remains a more
important structure of identity. For example, I am writing
this work as an Ilorin, brought up to experience Ilorin
Yoruba oral life (with the advantage of having other Ilorin
subgroup and ethnic experiences), and whatever it entails to
be an Ilorin is sufficient in defining me, the same way an Oyo
or Ijebu writer will ask to be seen as Oyo or Ijebu. This does
not detract from either of us any common definition used for
people who speak dialects of this same language and share
historical and cultural similarities. And so, as Achebe says,
even though the Biafran War became a powerful source of
mobilization and solidarity for the Igbo and their use of the
same name for their collective identity, that experience alone,
to use Achebe's words, "has very little to do with how deep it

is" (qtd. in Appiah, 1992: 177). Because the name *Biafra* has been used by the Igbos to describe themselves, and because all the people of Igboland speak the same language (with different dialects of it), what is new to them is the idea of a universal Igbo, or the idea of an Igbo nation that is different from their original clan-structure experience, and not the existence, the consciousness, or the depth of the identity of their being. Identity and collective or group recognition is therefore not new among the Igbo, as it is not among the Yoruba, Hausa, Fulani, or any one of the 400 language groups in Nigeria.

The concept of *b'ewe bape lara ose a di ose* discussed earlier in this chapter leads to the factors that help the intrinsic cultural plurality to thrive in Yoruba oral society. As a society of active orality, the entire community is exposed to constant oral performances in the marketplace, on the farm, at socioreligious ceremonies, and at village or town squares; and every member of the society grows up recognizing through songs, festivals, and oral narratives, the diversity of his community. The Yoruba people seem to have had the most urban African precolonial people (with Ife, Oyo, Ibadan, etc.). It is easy certainty to a Yoruba person, for example, that he, by the provision of the inherent Yoruba plurality culture, lives in a world of diversity where he can practice a religion different from the one practiced by his aunt, or that his village or town king can worship one day with a Sango adherent and the next day with an Ogun worshiper. Because he listens constantly to praise poetry performed by his mother/father or grandparent every morning when he pays them morning homage, and hears a different kind of poetry performed by neighboring young person, he knows that his community is made up of widely diversified lineages. In her own household she is praised as *Asabi*, one specially chosen [by her parents] to be born, two other children are praised as *Amasa*, one whom one comes to know and quickly runs away from, and as *Aduke*, one whom everyone rushes enthusiastically to please. He later realizes that praise names can be even more radically different, such as *Adenike* (from the royal family),

Ognnmola (from the household of Ogun worshippers), *Ayangbàmi* (from the family of oral singers or drummers). He may himself be a speaker of one of the many Yoruba dialects, and he realizes early that there are many varieties of his language, e.g., Egba, Ijebu, Oyo, Ekiti, Ijesa, Ife, Offa, Ilorin, and more. Because it is inherently plural, Yoruba culture has no problem accepting other diversities around it. I have heard a Yoruba professor suggest that the reason Islam and Christianity had no problem winning believers was because the typical traditional Yoruba person thought he was only adding to his list of gods and goddesses! This may explain why many Yoruba people who are Muslims and Christians still worship Yoruba deities (see Idowu 1962).

The active orality society has no need for laws and for government involvement to ensure a healthy interaction among the many cultures and beliefs within and around the community. The market is an open place, and every marketer opens his stall and advertises aloud in his dialect or language. When the oral singer sings in his community, nothing restricts how loud his voice gets or who hears him and who does not. He is not a television or radio that can be turned off or thrown out the window. The market woman's advertisement is not on the pages of newspapers or magazines that individuals can read silently and keep for themselve on their shelves. In an active orality society the culture is laid open; an active openness, accessible to all people according to given traditional principles. Yet the issue of identity is not a problem to the oral person.

Of course, there is a Yoruba identity, and the name *Yoruba* neither came with European colonization nor was it formed by the British colonial masters as was the name *Nigeria* as a country nor *Nigerian*, as a citizen name. A child may start to see himself as an Oyo; soon children of different dialects of the same Yoruba culture come to embrace each other and to proclaimed their Yorubaness while remaining their local selves: the Egba, Ijebu, Ekiti, Ijesa subidentities. An Ijebu Yoruba compromises nothing by sharing the diverse spaces of the Yoruba world with remaining Yoruba subgroups such as the Oyo or Egba Yoruba. Neither does a Yoruba person feel he compromises his Yorubaness by sharing the open market with a Nupe, Fulani, Hausa, Ebira, or Beriberi in his own domain.

In other words, cultural interactions and influences are not often seen as threatening in oral societies, since in all instances, the majority[4] oral culture survives, and in many instances nativizes cultural elements from contacts with minority groups.

But in many instances, the nativization process is adopted both ways: The majority nativizes elements from the minority and the minority from the majority. Often what is minority in a certain community becomes a majority in its own domain. A good example comes from Ilorin: a Yoruba-cum-Hausa-Fulani settlement in the early nineteenth century. It was reported that Ilorin's market was so big, and that traders from neighboring communities constantly came to sell their goods there (an American observer was reported to have described it as "one of the greatest centerpots of central Africa" (qtd. in Olaoye 1984: 4; I wonder how central Ilorin is in Africa?). In this situation, speakers of languages such as Nupe, Baruba, Hausa, Yoruba, and Fulfude, who formed the neighboring communities, participated in the Ilorin market. Being an oral culture market, its advertisements were in Yoruba; but there were advertisements also in many of these sister languages, and there could be different stalls for different language groups. The reality of this situation is that words, concepts, and terminology from one language group are acquired into another language group. But then such concepts, and terminology are nativized or indigenized such that they become members of their host languages' vocabularies. They assume positions as cultural and linguistic elements of their new setting. An example from the English language is the heavy borrowing in modern English, by which many foreign words are now counted as English language words. The modern English situation must also have been helped by an element of orality.

In any event, through oral performances, the process of indigenization or nativization of cultural elements occurs more rapidly. This is a process of "accommodation" of "difference" and/or "similarity," what I like to describe as "indigenizing difference" and/or "indigenizing similarity." In other words, both differences and similarities acquire positions as members of another oral culture. This is not anything near the "assimilation" through which the French colonial rulers expected Africans to shed their culture and become French citizens in thought, word, and deed. Indigenizing and nativizing[5] are processes where active orality makes possible a life of diversity within and outside ethnic existence. The advertisement songs in the market, the oral performances in the streets, community centers, farms, towns, and villages, etc., help ensure that cultural pluralism in active orality society is a positive event. No one is threatened or feels threatened, and no one loses his or identity identity.

This chapter continues the discussion of Yoruba as a highly diverse language and cultural group. However, it argues that similarities, rather than differences, are the hallmarks of its inherent cultural plurality. The chapter positions itself in arguing for an understanding of multicultural concepts in an active orality society such as the Yoruba's, concepts that definitely differ from those in New World societies. Using Ilorin Yoruba as an example, the next chapter discusses how, in an intrinsically culturally plural society, the people can easily retain their identity despite multilingualism and multicultural influences.

Chapter 5

RHETORIC OF SIMILARITY, INDIGENIZING DIFFERENCE

꧁꧂

I have thus far presented arguments for the inherently cultural plurality of the Yoruba. I hope I made it clear from the preceding chapters that differences in views and opinions, in cultural practices, or even in religion are not new to the Yoruba. The Yoruba say, *Bayi laase ni ile tiwa, eewo ibomiran*, meaning "'This way is how we behave in our house, is an abomination in another house/place!" This shows that Yoruba culture recognizes that not all practices and norms are universal, and a person must be ready to learn "behavior" all over again when he becomes a guest in a foreign culture.

I have also emphasized that the Yoruba orality society, which is very much alive in the twenty-first century, operates within sets of cultural values and traditions that have nourishing critical apparatus, such as *elaloro*, for engaging in, understanding, and appreciating of literary values. The various examples of Yoruba oral materials that we have discussed show the Yoruba people as holding strongly to their active orality status despite centuries of colonial and postcolonial influences from the West.

However, as the Yoruba people find their cultural and identity survival in the 21st Century, have they sufficiently explored the advantages of their orality society, its inherent cultural plurality, and the lessons so strongly taught in Yoruba folktales for confronting sociopolitical problems of the multicultural and multilingual Nigeria? One of the reasons for asking this question is that having previously presented the argument that colonial and postcolonial influences have not destroyed the ability of the contemporary Yoruba to know their culture, I want to end this chapter by discussing how much contemporary Yoruba elite have reflected in the ethics of their oral culture and applied them to their own lives.

Perhaps one thing I may have repeatedly emphasized in the previous chapters was the fact that the Yoruba orality culture focuses on similarities rather than differences when interacting with other cultures, and that this lends itself to a process of *indigenizing*, through which the Yoruba *nativizes* forms from "sister" oral cultures that may be construed as differences. Since the Yoruba culture already has its own set of pluralistic cultural practices, it would not be correct to think that the "fear" of allowing for more differences "bothers" it. By indigenizing differences, it only permits the basic characteristics of an orality society to take their course. As long as there is an interaction between two orality societies, *nativizing* and *indigenizing* the sister culture's sociolinguistic forms will always take place within each of the cultures involved. Yet, another point must be clarified. Can we then not assume that by *nativizing difference* the host culture is actually emphasizing the different identity of its sister culture rather than the similarities it shares with it? As I have stated before in this work, the emphasis on similarities in oral cultures, and in Yoruba oral tradition, for example, is not a "turning of a blind eye" to the reality that differences exist between cultures and among traditions. By nativizing difference, an African oral culture is utilizing its strategy for accepting those differences. In other words, it can be said that every orality society culture has realized that when differences are recognized, but not emphasized upon, let alone overemphasized, ideas about similarities will become the recurrent features of cultural polemics.

It is my conviction that *rhetoric of similarity* is deeply rooted in Yoruba culture. The logic here is simple. Since Yoruba culture is inherently diverse, its disparate views, its subcultures, and its many religions and worship processes are *united* through emphasis on *(the) similarities* among them. Tension is only logical if a culture as intrinsically plural as Yoruba always beats the drum of differences rather than that of similarities. Perhaps this is a value that the New World multicultural society can learn from the Yoruba active orality pluralist culture.

However, again, I am not so naive as to shy away from the truth that contemporary African elites have played too long by the game of differences (and often use the rhetoric of differences) that they acquired from their Western learning. For example, I myself has heard from a Yoruba elite about how different a person can be from other Yoruba people when that person belongs to a different political group from the majority of Yoruba, or how un-Yoruba one is for professing a religion, Islam or Christianity, that is not considered a "traditional" Yoruba religion. Contemporary Yoruba elites who think this way are, in my view, changing the basic feature of Yoruba logic. I was told by a member of Yoruba elite: "Oruko re yi naani [the problem is your name]!" Perhaps he/ she was inferring that because my name is *Abdul-Rasheed* (or *Rasidi*, as many will call me in my Ilorin home), an Islamic name referring to one of the Ninety-nine names of Allah (*Al-Rasheed*, meaning the Guide, and *Abdul-Rasheed*, worshiper/ servant of the Guide), my Yorubaness is automatically in doubt! As a doctoral candidate looking forward to resuming the professional life of a full-time teacher, I had asked for support from this Yoruba person in my efforts to find placement in an American university. I still do not know how my Muslim name would have been a problem in the late 1990s in a senior Yoruba professor's efforts to guide or help me in the process of securing a teaching position in America.

If a person is out to find differences among the Yoruba, i.e., to do exactly what this Yoruba elite has done, or what Kwame Appiah does in his *In My Father's House*, in differentiating Africans, i.e., Ghanaians, Botswanaians, etc., one will end up showing that several cultural practices in Ilorin and Iwo, two Yoruba communities with a strong Islamic presence in Nigeria, are not actually Yoruba, and that most Ilorin and Iwo people are Arabs, not Yoruba. This attitude of Western-minded Yoruba elites will only continue to lead to problems and cause tension, the kind of which we have discussed about contemporary New World multicultural societies.

Needless to say, this attitude is not limited to contemporary Yoruba elites. Several elites from other ethnic groups in Nigeria have also abandoned the fine active orality plurality tradition of accommodating difference. They now emphasize their differences instead of celebrate their similarities. Scholars trying to understand contemporary crises in Nigeria and Africa would be shortsighted in saying that it is a result of a tradition of the so-called constant wars among ancient African tribes! In my opinion, it is caused by the new waves of postcolonial bastardization of the inherent plurality of their African cultures. They have perfected division tactics, which they inherited from the colonial masters, and now they must reject other Africans based on ethnicity, religion, and perhaps even social class!

Since independence from Britain, Nigerians have fought a civil war caused by the attempts of Igbo-dominated Eastern Nigeria to secede from Nigeria, and from that time on, Nigeria has seen a succession of military coups in which every army brings in sets of ethnic loyalists to rule with the regime. Military regimes, at both local and federal levels, have ruled as if Nigeria was not a multicultural, multiethnic, and multireligious federation where, in an open market, every group explores its own great potential while also feeling like a solid part of the whole.

Perhaps it is this military take over of post-independent Nigeria and the discriminatory tradition of successive military administrations that caused and still causes many Nigerian elites to begin to abandon the *philosophy of similarities* so clearly inherent in our oral cultures. They would rather see themselves as people different from others and monopolize political power, often in favor of those who speak the same languages or belong to similar political linings or attend the same educational institutions as themselves. This is contrary to the orality values previously discussed.

I commented earlier on the marriage of inconvenience that is the colonial heritage of modern African states. I am unsure whether Africans, many decades after so-called independence from the colonial masters, have become accustomed to the colonial arrangement of a haphazard Westernized statehood or whether any solution can come from a reexamination of the colonial heritages in Africa, especially the cultural and sociopolitical ones. One thing is certain: African orality has more than enough ethics to show that it does not believe in the current games of "winner-takes-all" that have been very damaging to African peoples' lives. One would think that having a culture that emphasizes being one's brother's keeper, as we often see in most African folktales,[1] African leaders have enough cultural upbringing to be tolerant leaders. One would think Nigerian leaders, at least those of Yoruba heritage, would be good leaders for their people and work to create a nation in which its resources are used for the cause of peace, environmental balance, and the development of Nigeria and its people. Alas, Nigerian leaders are among the worst in the world when it comes to taking their duties with a sense of responsibility and with love for their people. It seems to me that a typical Nigerian leader, of any language group, knows his pocket first and foremost and perhaps has no knowledge of anything else.

Unlike the traditional tolerant attitude of the active orality culture, the practice today among contemporary Africans, Nigerians, and Yoruba is akin to what the Yoruba describe as *boba o pa, booba o jan lese*: meaning that "if you meet him kill him, if you do not meet him (throw and) hit him on the legs [so that he misses his steps and eventually falls down]." The issue, though, is that most of these behaviors are rampant among elites in various language groups, those who, after their initial oral cultural education through the folk and oral legendary tales and performances at home and in their villages and towns, have imbibed the Western culture of individualism whose preoccupation is more with "what I can get for myself" than with what can the Nigerian nation or my family or village or city achieve? Many of them have been abroad and, having been schooled in Western political ideologies, are eager to demonstrate their "strange" expertise in "strange ideologies."

Chapter 6

PLURALISM AND
THE NEW WORLD
FORMATIONS

※※

How do the multicultural formulations of the New World
societies, brought about by the transatlantic slave trade,
the pre- and post-World War II and the global century waves
of immigration, migration, placement, and displacement (see
Abu-Laban 1995: 98-9) compare with the inherently plural
and multiethnic realities of the Yoruba and indeed of African
oral societies? Nigeria alone has about four hundred exclu-
sively intelligible languages, and each language has many
dialects. What can the written, high-tech, and cyberspace
cultures of the late twentieth and early twenty-first century
West learn from indigenous cultures of Africa, specifically
from the concept and practice of Yoruba intrinsic cultural
plurality? Having lived and studied in Canada for four years
and now residing and teaching in the United States for over
a decade, and as a keen observer of and in some cases as par-
ticipant in the various multicultural activities of governments,
schools, community associations, and individuals, I am eager
to compare notes, in some detail, between what I recognize
as cultural pluralism in an active oral society of Africa and
the written culture of my current abode. As I teach in the

West, the questions I constantly answer include how the inherent cultural plurality of my African society compares with the Western multiculturalism and whether scholars are right to apply the Western concept of multiculturalism in discussing the active orality culture of the multiethnic Africa.

In the twenty-first century, Yoruba oral performances still show that Yoruba culture has not lost its identity, notwithstanding decades of Western influence on its spaces. In performative songs and poetry, oral festivals, and dramatic and narrative forms, the Yoruba continue to project their sociocultural lives. My intention here is to examine some Yoruba folktales and to define, within the scope of Yoruba orality, the idea of inherent pluriculture or cultural pluralism in an oral society. How does Yoruba cultural reality compare with contemporary multiculturalism in the New Worlds? The West, represented by New World societies, Canada and the United States, and Australia, Argentina, New Zeeland, etc., battles with multicultural conflict that results from a contest for ethnic nationalism. The New Worlds, which are "written societies," as I like to call them, live daily in hotbeds of ethnocultural tensions as different racial, language, and cultural groups continue the battle to retain their cultural identity while also cooperating with the general idea of a new nationhood. Ian Angus (1997: 143), summarizing what some critics consider the situation of such crisis, explains thus:

> It is notable that critiques of multiculturalism, both in Canada and elsewhere, almost always take this rhetorical form: "what's the point of stressing our differences? They're all in the past (or destructive, or irrelevant). What's important is that we're all Canadians (or Australians, or Argentinians, or Americans, etc.)." That is, multicultural affiliations are experienced as *competing with* national ones, which implies that they are seen as being in *the same domain of relevance.* It does seem that a weak sense of national identity was historically necessary for the practice of multiculturalism

> to appear in English Canada in its particularly
> strong form. (Pp. 143-44)

Written society's views of culture, nation, and identity are different from the common understanding of the same concepts in an oral culture such as that of the Yoruba. Culture, religion, and identity are major issues to an oral person, and the modern nation-state, though important, is not considered of greater significance. Rather, the Yoruba oral culture or ethnicity (like all others) demands respect from the modern nation-state, and this "respect" is not the type a Western person calls so; it is reverence and recognition and a more-than-life treatment. Before European colonization of Africa, there was no separation between state and culture, between identity and state, and between religion and cultural practices. The word used by the Yoruba to denote modern "government" is *Ijoba*, meaning "a collection or meeting of kings and chiefs." That shows that their idea of government is not what the postcolonial nation-state gives them as government. This reality continues strongly in most African traditions today, and Kwame Anthony Appiah's narrative about his late father's funeral is a good example. Apart from his father's will and the codicil appended to it about his wishes for his burial, and maybe the involvement of the church, every other element of that experience was completely oral, and even the Wesley Methodist Church was brought to kneel before the custodian of Ashanti's traditions (Appiah 1992: 181-92). Even though some modern African leaders and law makers may project the Western notion of nationhood onto their people, I can say boldly that an oral person feels that this is contrary to the reality of his existence. I also hasten to say that although Ian Angus's expectations about multiculturalism in New World societies are laudable, I doubt whether his definition of "multiculturalism as a social ideal" has contemporary Europe and America in mind or whether the "social ideal" of multiculturalism is ever attainable in, for example, English Canada:

> Multiculturalism as a social ideal is about how to
> conduct oneself in a society constituted by a pluri-
> cultural context and how to design a concept of
> national identity that is inclusive of the plurality
> of traditions. (Angus, p. 140)

Because New World societies are basically immigrant societies, the polemic surrounding multiculturalism in the West
might often be reduced to which ethnic group settles there
first or which race has the majority of a country's population. Raymond Breton (1989: 150) itemizes, starting with
the 1960s, the main reasons that promoted multiculturalism
in Canada:

1. Massive immigration: between 1945 and 1961, over
   two million legal immigrants entered Canada. This
   increased the weight of the non-British, non-French
   component of the population.
2. This period also witnessed rapid economic growth.
   The abundance generated had the effect of decreas-
   ing the saliency of class interest and consequently
   allowed other lines of social differentiation to come
   to the foreground.
3. A third phenomenon was the considerable expansion
   of the involvement of the state in all areas of social
   life. The state became considerably more activist, and
   it was virtually inevitable that its intervention would
   include the ethnocultural field.
4. Corresponding to the increase in state activism, there
   was a considerable increase in the sociopolitical mobilization of various social groups. The 1960s and early
   1970s was a period of great "social ferment," a phenomenon that occurred not only in Canada but in the
   United States, Europe, and other parts of the world.
5. Perhaps the phenomenon that had the most impact
   in putting ethnicity on the public agenda was the
   rise of a new Quebec nationalism and especially
   the emergence of the independentist movement in

that province. This movement forced a reconsideration of the character of Canadian society; it led the national elites to a reshaping of national institutions. This reconstruction process raised the question of the place of the "other ethnic groups" in the evolving Canadian configuration. The Royal Commission on Bilingualism and Biculturalism acted as the principal crystalizer in this collective *prise de conscience*.

6. The increased demographic weight and corresponding political importance of the non-British/non-French element in Canadian society and the rise of the independentist movement in Quebec increased the saliency for Canadian society of the demise of the British Empire. Canada could define itself less and less in relation to that empire. This was not a new phenomenon, but its reality imposed itself forcefully on the national consciousness at the end of World War II.

Basically in Canada and the United States, the debate is between English (Anglo-)-Canadians, Anglo-Americans and the Other; the Other being Africans, Indians, Russians, Ukranians, African-Americans, Mexicans; and this Other does not even include the aboriginals who are the original inhabitants of the so-called "New" World societies, and who, we may argue, are currently treated as less than Other in the debate. For example, in Canada, the issues have always centered around English Canada, French Canada, and even with these two groups the multicultural debate, as shown by Angus, has always been English Canada vs. the Other or French Canada vs. the Other, what they call "multiculturalism within [a] bilingual framework" (Angus, p. 141). Angus states further:

> The post-colonial phase of Canadian history has increasingly criticized privileging the British connection and asserted the multiple immigrant origins of all Canadians. As a consequence, there is a duality inherent in the popular term "ethnics" because of the conditions of its emergence. The

term "ethnics" can refer to all those of non-British origin, as it once did, meaning more or less "those who are not like us," or, to the extent that the privileged British connection fades, it can refer to the "ethno-cultural roots of whatever group," including English Canadians. (Pp. 141-42)

From Augus's observations we can clearly understand that the word ethnic in one of its meanings refers to the ethnocultural roots of any group. However, usage of the same word in contemporary Western multiculturalism parlance may have little respect for this meaning. For example, it is not often that English Canada refers to itself as *ethnic*. The word is beginning to seem disdainful, and now almost looks like the word always used for American Indian and African language groups in Western media: tribes or tribal people! *Ethnic* in the New World society today, as far as I can see, is beginning to mean the Other, as one may easily see in the course contents of Ethnic Studies programs in universities in North America. It is a power game, and the majority may be said to have redefined the word to mean "minority groups." If I may ask, can the term *ethnic*, with all its current seemingly derogatory significations,[1] continue to be used for all groups in the twenty-first century or has it finally stopped, for example, in Canada, to include the French-Canadian, and the Anglo-Canadian groups and henceforth solely used for the Others? Whatever happens to such a word in our global century, could the majority groups in the New World of this century, e.g, the English and the French Canadians and the Anglo-Americans, see themselves as Other in any possible way? To think that English Canada could easily be counted as the Other is simply a joke. However, two things could make this happen in Canada, but I strongly believe that neither is visible under today's sun. The first one is if other ethnic groups (two or three, not just one group) like the Indians, the Russians, the Ukranians, the Jews, the Chinese increase in number and become more populous than the Anglo-Canadians, then the Anglo-Canadians may begin to feel what it is to be a minority in Canada. Since there would then be a possibility for these ethnic groups to increase their representation in Parliament, they may easily constitute a majority in Her Majesty's government. The second way English Canadians could become the Other in Canada is if the Canadian Federal Parliament passes a bill by a two-thirds majority pronouncing English Canadians the "Other." Yes, it seems senseless to those who have the power to willingly commit a power suicide (see Goldenberg 1989: 137), to give up their privilege, doesn't it?

Yet, multiculturalism in New World societies is a creation of legislation and not a spontaneous or natural course of events. Today Hispanic Americans are growing in number and becoming a significant portion of the population of the United States, and calls are being made for the use of Spanish in American schools. However, the various pronouncements of American law makers—Republicans and Democrats— show that the United States Congress would never pass such a law that they already consider a "foolish" law, because in their thinking it would willingly make it possible for English America to become one of the Others in the 21st Century. Pat Buchanan and Bob Dole, both Republican Party presidential candidates in the 1996 presidential primary election, made the supremacy of the English language in America a campaign issue. For those who listened to the rhetoric of the Republican primary that year, it was as if the Spanish or foreign language issue was an imminent nuclear war against the United States of America! It was as if a siege were about to take place against the country by foreign immigrants and responsible politicians must take up arms against it. I doubt whether such politicians ever consider the fact that a large percentage of the current United States land mass was originally Mexican or whether they thought for a minute that the original languages of America was not English but Native American languages! It definitely did not seem to occur to them, and if it did they did not care, that Latino and Native Americans might be listening to their debates.

In 1997, when a United States county schools board passed a law recognizing Ebonics as a black language "for teacher's consideration in teaching," and not as a replacement of English as a language of instruction in schools, President Clinton, a Democrat, was the first to condemn it and to announce publicly the federal government's intention to frustrate or even block its implementation. This may be a valuable lesson to Latinos, i.e., that their predicted imminent majority population over blacks or African Americans in America may not help the Spanish language question in the United States. The Anglo-conformity, or assimilation wave, in America is not about to disappear, despite Peter Rose's (1989, 154-5) prediction of the reduction in "the salience of white ethnicity" in the year 2000. According to Rose "the principal tensions in 2000 will not be between Black and White in our society but between the White or Anglo community and the Hispanic ones" (p. 156). Listening now to Lou Dobbs, the conservative CNN anchor who often, and fraudulently in my opinion, describes his position as independent, has definitely declared such a war with his anti-Latinos immigrant rhetoric on television. The twenty-first century has brought about troups of vigilantes to the United States-Mexico border, and they see it as their patriotic duties to chase and arrest illigant immigrants and to turn them over to law enforcement. The marveric American politician John McCain of Arizona, who in 2008 initially supported a compromise bill that was meant to give amnesty to illegal immigrants who were already in the United States by providing them a sure way to citizenship after paying a penalty and learning the English language, was forced to jettison his position in order to get his party's nomination for president of the United States. Concervative politics in America post-2000 is now about protecting the American border, and while Rose's prediction of reduced tension between black and white in America did not entirely come to pass, there seems to be increased tentsion from 2006, which continued in 2008, between ultraConservative white people and Latinos. For one, President George W. Bush dramatically increased his Latino votes in his reelection for president in 2004. For the first time it was being predicted that Latinos might be breaking their ties to the Democratic party. It can be said therefore that the real tension between conservative whites and Latinos resurfaced in the latter part of the decade.

Yet, with Barack Obama winning the Democratic Party nomination for president of the United States, after a very close race against the former first lady, Sanator Hilary Clinton, and eventually going on to win the november 2008 presidential election, it might be easily said that American whites and blacks are enjoying some reduced tension between them right now. Race was used in the Conservatives' campaigns against Obama. National polls in 2008 showed that he enjoyed only marginal support among whites compared with the support enjoyed by his Republican counterpart, John McCain. The same 2008 polls, however, also showed that America was ready for a black president. I doubt if the answer would have been a yes if the polls had questioned whether America was ready for a Latino president. The increasing tension between Latinos and whites due to the heated immigration issue is definitely responsible. Yet, it is more of a reason with white conservatives than with white liberals. Another complicated race problem in American is the distrust between African Americans and Latinos. As was demonstrated during the 2008 Democratic party presidential primary, Latinos voted enmass for Hilary Clinton, helping her to win California and Texas, with polls indicating among other reasons Latinos' distrust of having an African American president. Yet such distrust cannot be compared to the racial tension between whites and racial minorities, as immediately Obama became the Democratic party nominee, over 80 percent of Latinos switched their support to him instead of supporting the Republican party nominee, John McCain.

There is a difference between the Western idea of multiculturalism or pluralism and what I call cultural pluralism in Africa. Active orality of Africa brings about a faster, an easier, and, in my opinion, more beneficial interaction of cultures than the written society of the West. For one, the orality cultures interactions are without any prompting or regulations by parliamentary legislation or a modern presidential interference. In Europe and in America, government intervention is necessary to ensure that multiculturalism thrives and to reduce multicultural tension. The point is that because the West is a written world, a cyberworld, and a high-tech world, cultural interaction cannot be left to "the forces of nature," as people interact more through the printed words than through physical contact. The electronic orality of the telephone, the radio, the television, and the Internet satisfies, in all respects, my definition of passive orality of the New World societies because it does not, in any way, help interpersonal and intergroup contacts nor does it compare to the face-to-face orality such as we have in the active orality cultures of, for example, Kenya or Uganda.

Through legislation, the American and or Canadian governments attempt, respectively, to "help" foster multiculturalism. Some of the ways in which multiculturalism is ensured in New World nations are:

1. LEGAL IMMIGRATION (as in USA and Canada, with the American government even having a lottery program aimed at encouraging immigration to the country).
2. EDUCATION.
3. CULTURAL CELEBRATION (multicultural days and events, etc., like Heritage Days in Edmonton, Alberta, or like Taste of Chicago, in Chicago, Illinois).

As we can understand from Breton's summary, cited earlier in this chapter, the 1967 report of the Royal Commission on Bilingualism and Biculturalism in Canada principally encouraged the introduction of a multicultural policy in 1971, aiming at assisting non-Anglo- and non-Franco-Canadians to "integrate" into Canadian society. However, it must be emphasized that whereas the idea was supposed to help minority ethnic Canadians retain their culture, it was, more than anything else, intended to "assimilate" them into one of the dominant Canadian cultures, i.e., English or

French. This is how Huguette Labellé (1989) summarizes the major objectives of the Canadian multicultural policies:

1. To permit cultural groups to retain and foster their identity.
2. To assist cultural groups to overcome barriers to their full participation in Canadian society.
3. To promote creative exchanges and interchanges among all Canadian cultural groups.
4. To help newcomers acquire at least one of the official languages.

The objectives of the Canadian government are largely similar to those of the United States government in many of its multicultural policies (see Rose, pp. 153-57). On language, as seen in objective no. 4 above, Canada seems to encourage immigrants to forego their languages for one of the two Canadian official languages, either English or French, and to take up a so-called Canadian identity. It is therefore only logical to see that the immigrants are not encouraged, nor are they able, to maintain their culture where they are unable to maintain their language. Just as Jean Burnet observes, "a culture could not live unless the language that was its essential expression remained rich and vital" (p. 14). Yet, a Canadian prime minister was reported to have said, in 1971:

> "[A]lthough there are two official languages, there is no official culture, nor does any ethnic group take precedence over any other. No citizen or group of citizens is other than Canadian, and all should be treated fairly." (Qtd. in Labelle, p. 2; also see Abu-Laban 101)

There is no doubting the government's intention in Canada, in the United Sates, and in other countries of the New World, to make the non-British immigrants (and non-French ones in Canada) "feel at home" in their new societies. Every year large sums of money are spent on programs to help immigrants adjust to the life of their new communities. The question is: Are those "adjustment programs" the type that will help the immigrant retain his or her culture and identity? The following is how Huguette Labelle describes such programs:

> There are, of course, limits to the activities of the multicultural program, less perhaps through the size of its staff and its budget than through the need to move prudently in concert with community advice. Nevertheless, a number of other interesting activites have been launched. Assistance has been given to the Canadian Broadcasting Corporation (CBC) for a training program for members of visible minorities. A study was made on audience reaction to the CBC drama "Reasonable Force" about the harassment of a Sikh family. The Ontario Federation of Labour received a grant for an advertising program on the theme "Racism Hurts Everyone." The National Film Board received financing to produce a film by a black film maker about Caribbean Canadians in North York. Funding has made it possible for many multicultural organizations to carry out media sensitization seminars. An innovative police training program has been conducted as a pilot project in Vancouver, and an international seminar is being planned on policing in multicultural and multiracial communities. The Canadian Jewish Congress has received funds to develop a legal-aid manual for community groups combating racism. (Labelle, p. 5)

Despite all the monies, all the efforts, and all the laws or policies, multiculturalism in New World societies remains tension ridden, minority ethnic groups struggle to assert their identities, and dominant groups work hard to retain their perceived national identity (i.e., English and French identities in Canada, English in the USA) rather than be open to multiethnic and cultural identities that one might expect in a society that calls itself multicultural. But multiculturalism in the New World means "many cultures with one language." That is what these countries have provided in their many multicultural laws and policies.

In other words, these policies have achieved basically what the Western multiculturalism intends them to achieve, not plurality but singularity or difference; not mutual respect, but disagreements and cultural tension between the dominant group(s) and the Other ethnic groups. In Canada and the United States in 1998, opposition political parties—e.g., the Reform Party in Canada and the Republican Party in the United States—constantly criticized their countries' immigration policies, and some anti-immigration activists in the two countries even called for a freezing of immigration for a certain number of years.

I have personally participated in Heritage Day presentations in some Edmonton and suburban public schools for four years, and every time I spoke about my culture to the kids I became more convinced that multiculturalism in the West is only about the rhetoric of difference. I became more and more certain that arguments such as Bisoondath's in *Selling Illusions: The Cult of Multiculturalism in Canada* (1994) is winning the day rather than losing it. Angus paraphrases Bissoondath's main contentions that

> he has personally been ghettoized and that Canada has deprived itself of a national identity as a result of multiculturalism. "To pretend that one has not evolved, as official multiculturalism so often seems to demand of us, is to stultify the personality, creating stereotype, stripping the individual of uniqueness: you are not yourself, you are your group." (Angus, p. 145)

Basically, therefore, multiculturalism in New World societies is about differences, not similarities. Because of the forces of "individual personality" that Bisoondath refers to above, multiculturalism in the West continues to be defined, notwithstanding what Angus wishes for (see pp. 144-6), by the modernist drive for individualism and by Western capitalist ideals. In terms of the capitalist ideal, important parts of the requirements for immigration to Canada include the amount of money the immigrant brings and/or the amount of formal learning he has attained, thus continually drawing the best brains and riches out of the Old Worlds and demonstrating the capitalistic ferocity of the New World societies. Regarding issues of individualism, similarity, or difference, the following narration about a Canadian Broadcasting Corporation (CBC) television discussion on multiculturalism in Canada is noteworthy:

> A CBC television news special on multiculturalism in 1994 insisted on the same rhetoric. At the beginning of the show, the moderator described multiculturalism as being about "acceptance, accommodation and, of course that most Canadian concept of all, compromise" and went on to refer to "what many believe multiculturalism should be: a search for our similarities, not a promotion of separateness." The important word here is "not." It is this little word that rejects the possibility that multiculturalism might be a search for both our similarities and differences, that it might be a way of working out within our own social and political history the dialectic of "identity and difference," within which all social identity operates. It must be recalled that this rhetorical position is not merely that of a contributor to the debate. It is articulated by the moderator prior to his turning to commentators and remains as a structuring assumption throughout. Later, when Harron Siddiqui, editor of the *Toronto Star*, was trying unsuccessfully to escape the logic imposed by the rhetoric of opposition, the moderator asked if he agreed with the statement of one of his opponents that multiculturalism "is about separateness, not about similarity." Various positions were debated, but the assumptions of rhetoric of opposition were, if not exactly mandatory, impos-

sible to question or reject within the confines of
the show. (Angus, p. 145)

It is impossible to avoid the issue of difference or sep-
arateness while discussing contemporary Western multiculturalism. The practicality of multiculturalism in New World
societies, as far as my own experience in Canada has shown
me, is that even young people in high school think of differences, rather than similarities, and act out the tension
that they have perhaps unconsciously experienced whenever
multiculturalism is a subject of discussion in their homes,
with their parents, or on the television. They have been fed
with so many stereotypical ideas that their minds have been
prepared to believe that other cultures are like bad air that
pollutes their "pure" civilizations. This is especially true about
Africa and ideas some of them hold that those people who
"live on trees" have hardly any "decent" lives outside of interacting with animals, and thus behave as if they themselves
are animals. A good example comes from one of the schools
where for more than three years I gave talks and made presentations on Nigerian culture. The school is an Alberta
public school called La Pointe School, Beaumont, and most
of my presentations were to grade seven students, taking
place every year for between ten and twelve classes, with each
class containing an average of twenty students. I was always
astonished by the amount of interest the students showed in
hearing my cultural talk and in participating in my folktale
sessions. Perhaps I learned the most from the kind of questions they repeatedly asked me, and in more than three years
of meeting different students, many of those questions never
changed: Why did you come to Canada? Will you go back to
your country? What kind of food do you eat in Nigeria? Do
lions (sometime elephants) hear your language, and can you
hear theirs? How do about 400 language groups live together?
What is the common form of greeting in Nigeria? Is Yoruba
(sometimes Hausa, Igbo) a language just like English?

I tried my best to answer these questions by explaining
the inherent commonalty among people, and how Nigerians

come to Canada and Canadians go to Nigeria, although for different purposes. However it has always been clear to me that what their minds have been prepared to hear, certainly not by their school but by their homes and by society at large, are answers resulting from differences between them as Canadians and myself as a Nigerian.

In a rural school, I understand why the population of non-white students is insignificant, but the point is that virtually all the classes I attended had a number of nonwhite Canadians. Being immersed in a community just a few kilometers away from Edmonton,[2] it is certain that the students in La Pointe School are not unfamiliar with the multiethnic face of Canada, and that although I am a Nigerian, I may have taken up permanent residency in Canada. Asking, I realized that the students knew well that their parents were British, American, or Scottish, etc. Once in another Edmonton school in 1996, I asked a black grade eight student where he came from and he said to me: "My parents are from Ghana, but I am a Canadian." I got the same answer from another student, grade seven, in the same school, except that her mother was a white Canadian. I was impressed by these students' sense of Canadian identity, but I wondered in my mind how the multicultured and the so-called hybrid are treated by the other white students, mainly Anglo-Canadians. In other words, the student with the Ghanaian mother and father I consider multicultural; and the one with Ghanain black father and white Canadian mother, hybrid.

Certainly this type of situation is limited among the Yoruba, especially in Yoruba oral communities. It is possible to see cross-racial marriages between the Yoruba and the English or French among middle-class Yoruba, in Nigerian Universities and business communities, etc., but such marriages do very little to change or influence changes in oral communities. In Kwame Appiah's book *In My Father's House*, we are not told what changes Kwame Anthony Appiah's mother, a white Briton married to a Ghanaian, brought about in the Asante community into which she is married. Hardly is her name mentioned in any of the controversies following her husband's death; rather, "we want to keep mother out of this" is the song that seems to come repeatedly from her children's mouths (pp. 181-192). In Appiah's Preface to the book, the first time he refers to his mother is in relation to her garden, "my mother's garden" (p. vii), and later the writer shows how his mother actively interacted with the oral community:

> In our house, my mother was visited regularly by Muslim Hausa traders from what we called (in the phrase that struck my childhood ear as wonderfully mysterious, exotic in its splendid vagueness) "the North." These men knew she was interested in seeing and, sometimes, in buying the brass weights the Asante had used for weighing gold; goldweights they had collected from villages all over the region, where they were being sold by people who had no use for them anymore, now that paper and coin had replaced gold dust as currency. And as she collected them, she heard more and more of the folklore that went with them; the proverbs that every figurative goldweight elicited; the folktales, *Ananseasïm*, that the proverbs evoked .... We loved the stories--my sister now read the ones that my mother has published to my nephews in Gaborone and in Lagos; my godchildren read them here in America--and we grew to love the goldweights and the carvings that the traders brought. (Pp. vii-iii)

That his mother collected and published Asante folktales is strong evidence of her interaction with the people and of the "nativization" process she went through into the Asante, her husband's culture. There are examples of similar situations in which whites have undergone similar processes in the Yoruba oral community. Perhaps the best example is that of an Austrian, Suzanne Wenger (1915-2009), who was actually initiated into Yoruba spirituality, became a worshipper of Yoruba gods of *Obatala* and *Alajere*, and plays an important role as *Iya Osun*, chief priestess, in the traditional *Osun Osogbo* annual festival (see Na'Allah, 1995: 103-4). Not only did Wenger become an indigene of the Osogbo oral community, her artistic creations were "nativized." Although Appiah's mother did not do as much as Wenger, she did what many whites who live in African active orality communities do, and the oral performers responded to her in kind, as any traditional oral culture will treat any woman or man interested in an oral performance according to relevant traditional custom. In the same vein, Appiah and his sisters, though products of white-black mixed marriages, cannot be described as hybrids. Appiah demonstrated in his book how Asante he is, far from the "hybridity" of my earlier Canadian example, incidentally also of a Ghanaian father. What the oral culture made of Kwame Appiah, thousands of pages of written cultural texts, including actively reading stories such as the ones Appiah's godchildren read in America, can never make a child born of African and white American parents residing in America or Canada, although those children remain evidence of American and Canadian multiculturalism in the New World societies in which they live.

There are so many similarities in oral cultures that what happens among the Yoruba could easily happen among the Asante or the Ga in Ghana or the Zulu in South Africa. In my Yoruba oral world, an "active orality" world, people "see" similarities and commonalties in their assessment of plurality, and I believe that this is so in many active African orality cultures. However, I am surprized, for example, that Kwame Appiah (1992) imposes a strange "multicultural" doctrine in his discussion of African culture. He says that, "nothing should be more striking for someone without preconceptions than the extraordinary diversity of Africa's peoples and its cultures" (24). Yet, his example is his visit to Botswana, where, he says, the landscape, "the material culture," and the men's dresses were unfamiliar to him (24). I believe that Appiah, in noticing the differences, had preconceptions and was practically out to look for differences rather than for similarities. He says later in that chapter:

Compare Evans-Pritchard's famous Zande oracles, with their simple questions and their straight-forward answers, with the fabulous richness of Yoruba oracles, whose interpretation requires great skill in the hermeneutics of the complex corpus of verses of Ifa; or our own Asante monarchy, a confederation in which the king is primus inter pares, his elders and paramount chiefs guiding him in council, with the more absolute power of Mutesa the First in nineteenth-century Buganda; or the enclosed horizons of a traditional Hausa wife, forever barred from contact with men other than her husband, with the open spaces of the women traders of southern Nigeria; or the art of Benin--its massive bronzes--with the tiny elegant goldweight figures of the Akan. Face the warrior horsemen of the Fulani jihads with Shaka's Zulu impis; taste the bland foods of Botswana after the spices of Fanti cooking; try understanding Kikuyu or Yoruba or Fulfude with a Twi dictionary. Surely differences in religion ontology and ritual, in the organization of politics and the family, in relations between the sexes and in art, in styles of warfare and cuisine, in language—surely all these are fundamental kinds of differences? (P. 25)

There is no doubt about the many levels of diversity in Africa, and the examples cited by Appiah are valid. Yet, the rhetoric he has adopted in discussing African diversity, it seems to me, may be better suited for the Western discourse of multiculturalism or diversity than the African one.

Chapter 7

THROUGH A MIRROR
OF DIFFERENT EYES

Because I was white,
It's almost a celebrity status
　　Dr. Lesley McCullough (CBC Radio 1, Edmonton,
　　"Mid-day Express," April 14, 1998, 12 noon to 2pm)

Don't care where you come from
As long as you're a black man, you're an African
No min'your nationality
You have got the identity of an African ...

No min'your complexion
There is no rejection, you are an African
Cos if your 'plexion high, high, high
If your'plexion low, low, low
And if your 'plexion in between
You're an African
　　Peter Tosh on his album, *African*

Listening to a Canadian Broadcasting Corporation (CBC) radio program on 14 April 1998, I heard a recent visitor to Malawi, a white female doctor, discuss how her being white made her a celebrity among Malawians. She said everyone greeted and hailed her on her way to and from the hospital where she worked. She said that among the greatest satisfaction of her visit was the sense of appreciation of Malawians who filled up her bags with mangos and oranges each day before she went home.

Listening to the account, I felt it was an interesting way of interpreting being a "white" visitor in Africa! What actually attracted me to her discussion was her initial assertion on the program that the idea of a woman medical practitioner was obscure to the Malawians. According to her, it was because there were two previous women doctors that the Malawians gradually learned to accept women as doctors, and that this "fact" eased whatever difficulty she might have faced as a woman doctor in the Malawian community. In a discussion with me later in the month,[1] McCullough said that one morning, in her presence, a female[2] tutor was introduced to the congress of the Central Church of African Presbyterian and the Malawians' "jaws hit the floor." In other words, they could not believe that a woman could occupy a position that would bring her so close to their priest let alone to the office of the priest itself. She contended that the new female tutor was a church minister in Canada but had to settle for a tutorship position in Malawi because the idea of a female minister was still strange to the community.

In many respects, Misuzi, Malawi, qualifies as a community of what I have termed in this book an "active orality" community, because most of its people depend mostly on the oral forms in communication, in literary expression, and in many other aspects of their lives. Natural or traditional African medicine is an active alternative to the orthodox Western medicine provided at the government hospital, and as in many communities of sub-SaharanAfrica, the majority of the people in Misuzi first resort to traditional medicine; only a few go to the hospital. Even those who go to Western hospitals usually start with traditional treatment from local herbalists before they consider going to the modern hospital.

Lesley McCullough is Canadian, and at the time of my discussion with her, she was living and working in Calgary, in the Province of Alberta, at the University of Calgary Hospital. Her interest in Malawi started during a discussion she had with one of her friends who had worked in the tropical African nation. She decided to go there herself, spending a little over a month in a Malawian northern regional capital called Misuzi starting in February 1998. The hospital where she worked was fairly large, with about four hundred beds, received funding from UNICEF as well as the Malawian government. The majority of the people in the region speak Timbuka and Titewa, and very tiny minority of the people, to the effect of 3 percent, also speak English.

I must say that I was disappointed with McCullough's misconception of traditional Africa and her claim that Africans she encountered had no concept of women medical practinioners or women priests. Whereas women in the West might not have been considered a complete "human being" for ages and only got the right to vote like their male counterparts in the early twentieth century, African women have always been accorded places of importance in many professional, cultural, and socioeconomic practices in Africa, including in the health and healing areas. In local Yoruba and Hausa communities, for example, women and men feature as herbalists, traditional African medicine producers, health administrators and managers, etc. In fact, in many African cultures women alone have specialized in child delivery and have provided services as nurses, midwives, and traditional pediatricians.

Indeed, colonial intervention in Africa was responsible for introducing a foreign system of medical education and practice where medicine became a male sanctuary. It must have seemed counterintuitive for many Africans to witness strange realities in colonial hospitals and clinics such as men intruding on pregnant women's privacy and prodding the mothers' genitals in the name of child delivery. It would be interesting to do research into how women in colonial Malawi, for example, reacted to the idea of opening themselves up to men who were not their husbands when hitherto they wouldn't have considered allowing their own brothers to intrude on them.

Again I think McCullough's interpretation of Malawian hospitality is precarious, as I strongly believe that the people's kindness towards her was simply a reflection of their culture. In many African cultures, a guest is like a king or queen to their hosts, as the hosts would leave their rooms for their guests if there is no guest room and put their guests' welfare above their own. The Malawians would have done the same as they did for the white doctor as they would for a medical doctor from Nigeria or Egypt. And in my view, it wouldn't have mattered whether it was a male or female doctor. But in a way the enthusiasm with which McCullough reenacted her Malawian experiences and the immediacy she brought to it on the radio program shows autobiography as a reperformance of the individual's life. The excitement and momentariniety that came through McCullough's voice as she told her story feature in the mind of every writer of an autobiography and enlivens the hand and pen with which he or she reperforms his/her experiences on paper. In other words, what excites me in autobiography is the opportunity to perform one's life experience all over again and to write out one's life on paper or to talk about it on radio or to stage it on public forums. I very much like how Ien Ang describes autobiography as a private act:

> If, as Janet Gunn has put it, autobiography is not conceived as "the private act of a self writing" but as "the cultural act of a self reading," then what is at stake in autobiographical discourse is not the narcissistic representation of the subject's authentic "me," but the narrative construction of a subject's social location through the active interpretation of experiences that one calls one's own in particular, "worldly" contexts, that is to say, a reflexive positioning of oneself in history and culture. In this respect, I would like to consider autobiography as a more or less deliberate, rhetorical construction of a "self" for *public*, not private purposes: the displayed self is a strategically fabricated performance, one which stages

> a *useful* identity, an identity which can be put to
> work. It is the quality of that usefulness which
> determines the politics of autobiographical dis-
> course. ("On Not Speaking Chinese," pp. 3-4)

Lesley McCullough's interpretations of her encounters in
Malawi, however, show that autobiography can suffer from
the narrator's misconception of his or her own life experiences. Therefore, the important issue in autobiographical text
should not be whether or not the writer or speaker is the sole
authority of his/her own life experience, but whether such
an experience is properly understood and interpreted by the
narrator. In other words, an autobiography needs informed
criticism to be acceptable and may desire a critical revision in
order to be authentic. The whole idea that Malawians turned
Dr. McCullough into a celebrity because of her race or the
color of her skin is totally inauthentic. It is like her account
of an encounter with her Canadian friend, also in Malawi,
who claimed that Malawians believe that when they walk
beside whites (medical doctors I suppose) "your intelligence
seem to flow into them,"[3] If she were to understand Malawian culture properly she would have been aware that her
hosts would have behaved similarly to a Ghanaian, Indian, or
Mexican doctor, and that the Malawians action has nothing
to do with transferring any intelligence. Such misconcep-
tions lead to the conclusion that there are experiences the
autobiographer must revisit, reassess, and revise.

McCullough's discussion of being white in Africa leads
me to my own experience of being a black visitor in the
Caribbean. When I realized that I was going to visit Grenada
for about three weeks starting at the end of December 1997,
a few things came to my mind about the Caribbean country.
I had learned and thus remembered that America invaded
it sometime in the early eighties. Although I wasn't able
to even recall the specific date of the invasion, I estimated
that I was an undergraduate student at the university of
Ilorin, Nigeria. I remembered that Ronald Reagan was the
American invader president. The whole idea of a country of

over two hundred million people invading another one of a mere seven or eight hundred thousand recurred to me after I arrived in Grenada. It suggested a mighty elephant flexing its muscles over a molecule that is visible only through the use of a powerful microscope. I knew that Grenada had a majority black population, a couple of hundred Indians, and a much smaller number of white resettlers. Like North and South American blacks, I knew that the Grenadian blacks' ancestors were forcibly brought across the ocean for slave work on the Caribbean plantations, and that many of them were later brought to settle in the Caribbean after slavery (what Jamaica Kincaid would call "dumped there as human rubbish"). No indigenous African languages are spoken in Grenada. Therefore, colonial influence continues to dictate their contemporary language and cultural practices. I knew that as a former British colony Grenada was English speaking, but I also realized that, like most African countries, the nation also had been kicked around like a soccer ball by a few other colonial masters[4] and might have multiple language influences on its form of English language.

Lesley McCullough's perception of being white in Africa brings me to my own understanding of my feelings of being defined as a black person during my visit to Grenada. We both were hailed in our respective places of visit. There are, however, major differences between these two situations, principal among which were that McCullough was white among a black population in Africa, while I was black among blacks in the Caribbean. On 1 January 1998, I landed in Grenada via Barbados and was greeted by a huge population of black men and women in airports, and I began to see again, as I did in Nigeria, a sea of black heads and a visible white minority. Most of the black people I met greeted me, some with a huge smile, some with a nod of approval. I smiled back and also nodded mutual approval.

My first week in St. George's, the Grenadian capital city, was very interesting. I was most of the time in my traditional Nigerian dress. I like my African clothes a lot and would even wear them occasionally in winter in Edmonton, Alberta (of course with several layers of underwear). But here I had a true dressing festival in the first week of my first journey to a clearly tropical climate in more than three years. I was in my Nigerian *dan dogo*[6] dress five out of the seven days a week. Whenever I had a shirt and trousers on, a common English dress worn in Grenada, and as long as I did not open my mouth to speak, black Grenadians' reactions and responses to me was not different to their reactions to their fellow black Grenadians: simple goodwill, brotherhood, approval. However, as soon as I spoke to anyone, the music immediately changed. The first question was: "Where are you from?" or "Are you from Africa?" Yes, I spoke English, but I was told there that my English had an accent. And true to the admonition I had recieved before coming to Grenada, I myself had some difficulties understanding the rather fast-paced spoken Grenadian English. With those questions I easily realized that to them, mine too stood out, as the moon stands out in the night sky. And my answers were always, "Oh, yeah. I'm from Nigeria. But I live in Canada," and sometimes only, "Nigeria."

Whenever I wore my *dan dogo* the reaction was entirely different. They already concluded I was from Africa. Some even simply asked, "Nigerian?" One day I was sitting with my wife at a corner on a major St. George's street, opposite the Grantell (Grenadian Telephone) main office, both of us in Nigerian attire. One Grenadian male, of about thirty-six years old, came over to us and asked, "Are you black conscious?" Well I knew he meant well as he shook my hands and had a warm smile on his face, but his question was strange to me. I knew about the Black Conscious Movement of the sixties, which also served as a backbone for many African people such as members of the Negritude movement who were interested in promoting black culture around the world. However, no one before that day had ever confronted me with a question such as Grenadian's. On further inquiries he said he was a Rastafarian, and that black consciousness was Rastafarians' main philosophy. "Well, I am a Muslim; and I celebrate my black culture, but it doesn't matter to me whether a person is black, brown, or white, because in Islam it doesn't matter at all," I finally responded. In calling myself a Muslim I was indeed one, and mearly stating a fact, not out to satisfy an ideological need of the moment. Identity is about one's life, belief, focus, and peace of mind, and one may have many identities all at the same time, though some identities cannot go together. One may be a Muslim and an Indian, but one can't be a Muslim and a Hindi in India for example. A person may not be a Christian or a Muslim and an atheist at the same time. Yet the claim by a Yoruba king claiming that he takes or belongs to all the religions of all his people is very complex. It is doubtful if what he truly means is taking the religious identity of every one of his subjects in his real-life daily living other than his ceremonial performances.

Talking about my Muslim identity reminds me about my discussion of Akeel Bilgrami's take on identity in another forum (Africanity 2009). In one instance he talked about what he calls Muslim moderates and the conflict they do or do not have in their hearts (see "What Is a Muslim?" 821-42). Yet, some quick statements here on Bilgrami's assertions may be in order before I continue with my reperformance of my traveler or tourist life in Grenada. Says Bilgrami (824):

> The complexity of this pair of questions does not lie merely in the conflict between a minority of Islamic absolutists (or "fundamentalists" as they are sometimes misleadingly called) and a far larger class of Muslim moderates who oppose their vision of an antisecular polity based on Islamic personal and public law (Sahria). There is widespread today a more interesting conflict *within* the hearts of moderate Muslims themselves, a conflict made the more excruciating because it is not always explicitly acknowledged by them. This is the tension generated by their opposition to Islamic absolutism on the one hand and, on the other, their faith in a religion that is defined upon detailed commitments with regard to the polity,

commitments that Islamic absolutists constantly
invoke to their own advantage.

It is interesting that Bilgrami, a confessed Communist or
at least one who had "grown up in a home dominated by
the views of an irreligious father, and ... had ... adopted the
customary aggressive secular stance of those with communist leanings" (822), knows the minds of Muslims, moderate
or not, or that he manages to enter the so-called moderate Muslims' heart and knows what conflicts they have in
them or about why they would not cause radical changes
in a Muslim/Islamic environment. Most of his conclusions
about Muslims in that article are colored by his own personal
ideologies and experiences and his wide-ranging imaginings
that lead him to fake an Islamic identity for himself. As a
Muslim myself I know that my views are informed by my
understanding of the Qur'an and the Hadith. The definition he gives to "Islamic absolutism," to which he said his
imaginary moderate Muslims are opposed, is interesting.
From what I tried to explain to the Grenadian Rastafarian, absolutism in Islam can only be defined in terms of the
omnipotence and omnipresence of God; the idea of the five
pillars of Islam; the idea that God is One and had no child,
and that neither is God begotten (see the Qur'an, chapter
"Al-Ikhlas;" and my paper, "Is *Al-Mukhlit* a Critically Useful
Term to the Islamic Features in African Literature?"); and in
terms of the claim by Islam to be the religion for all humanity. Absolutism in Islam cannot be defined by the fact that a
particular Muslim holds an absolute or a moderate view of
certain Islamic doctrine. Individuals act according to their
own understanding or interpretation of the Qur'an and the
Hadith, and every one, if it might be said, is absolute in his
or her own convictions.

My Grenadian questioner said he had once converted to
Islam and now reverted back to Rastafarianism because he
was convinced Rastafarianism was the ideal religion for black
people. He addressed me by the word "brother," the same as
most Grenadian males I encountered called me throughout my

short visit. He said to me as he was leaving me, "Brother, please try to be black conscious. Good to see you. I hope I'll go to Africa some day." While he knew from our dress that we weren't Grenadians, he, like other Grenada males, had already determined my identity and based on that had chose what to call me.

Throughout my three weeks' stay in Grenada, I was never confronted with a search for identity or with a feeling of "not belonging." I was never allowed to have to make such a search or to engage in such a thought. Could it be because my visit was a short one? Would my experiences be different if I had been an African woman and not an African male? For example, if Dr. Lesley McCullough had been a white male doctor, would her treatment by Malawians be different, or would her interpretation of a Malawian hospitality be different from the one she recounted?

There are more questions! Ien Ang's one-day visit to China was quite similar to my own visit to Grenada in some paradoxical ways. We were both visiting peoples of our ancestry—she was visiting Chinese people in homeland China, and I was visiting black people in the Black Caribbean. The responses she had were complete opposite to mine. Despite her many efforts to gain recognition from Lan-lan, the twenty-seven-year old Beijing Chinese woman who was their tourist guide, she said, "An instant sense of alienation took hold of me" ("On Not Speaking Chinese," p. 3), because Lan-lan did not show any recognition or acknowledgment of Ang's Chineseness. She said she was forced by her experiences in China to "repeatedly [find] myself looking at this minute piece of 'China' through the tourists' eyes" (ibid.).

Repeatedly for me, I found that each time anyone asked me about my visit to Grenada my answer has been that it was like home, like going home to Nigeria. Perhaps what strikes me most about Ien Ang's and my own visits to "our peoples," respectively, is the huge difference in the reaction of those peoples to each of us. Unlike myself, Ang was forced to revisit the question of her own identity as a diapora Chinese; she was forced to consider the challenges of not being at home as a Chinese and was forced to explain what she calls the "apparent oddity" of "Why then don't I speak Chinese" (ibid.). As a last gesture of sisterhood to Lan-lan, Ang talked to Lan-lan, apparently in English, but only seemed to have compounded her problem. Said she:

> I said goodbye to Lan-lan and was hoping that she would say something personal to me, an acknowledgment of affinity of some sort, but she didn't. (p. 3)

Unlike the affinity clearly demonstrated with me by my black "brother" in Grenada, Ang was totally ignored by her Chinese "sister" in China. Obviously there was a difference in our (Ang's and my) two situations, as both my Grenadian brother and myself are at the moment outside the motherland (Africa) and can thus be called African diasporans. We may just be demonstrating the solidarity of a common African ancestry from the Diaspora where we currently live or at least met. I am not entirely sure if he knew that I was not living in Africa at that time, for all he thought it might be that I was visiting from Africa! Ang and Lan-lan did not share this sentiment at the time they are meeting. For one, Lan-lan does not likely understand what it is to be in the Diaspora and could not mobilize any such feeling to respond in solidarity with Ang. Yet, the interpretation of our hosts's (if we can call them that) actions or inactions would be different because of so many other factors: For example, one is motivated by ideological or religious reasons, and the other seems likely to have nothing of such as a motivation.

I conclude this chapter by raising more questions, as it would be out of character to reach a conclusion in an autobiographical piece about matters one has not or may not experience. The Grenadan shares some important similarities with Ang: He is a permanent African diasporan being of slave ancestry and therefore would be a stranger when he visits Africa. He speaks no African language, although recognizing African-Grenada shared colonial experience, he would easily find people who understand English if he visits

Anglophone Africa, but he might go to some places in Africa where no one would understand what he says! I remember that my Grenadan brother expressed his wish to visit Africa someday. How would he confront or be confronted by the identity issue while in Africa? Would Peter Tosh's songs about being an African, no matter where one comes from, prevail? Would other African brothers and sisters hail him and shower him with nods of recognition and approval, or will they call him a Yankee?

Has Lesley McCullough, if she has repeated her visit to Malawi as she wanted to do, changed her opinions about the implication for her white identity in Malawi? Would my own opinions and experience change when I make another visit to Grenada or to any of the other Caribbean countries? Would Ang ever want to visit China again?

More questions still, Could it be that the reaction or lack of reaction that Ien Ang got from Lan-lan was because it was inadvertently believed that she herself had determined her own space and identity by traveling with a majority of white tourists? Says she, "Our group of twelve consist(s) mainly of white, Western tourists—and me" ("On Not Speaking Chinese," p. 1). Would Lan-lan had acted more reciprocally to her if she had gone there alone and had been the only tourist she guided on that visit? Or would Lan-lan's actions be different if all the tourists had been Indonesian or Italian Chinese?

A few days before I left St. George's, Grenada, I was featured on a life program on MTS television station, and it was broadcast simultaneously on the company's radio station. A Grenadan who watched the show later asked me whether I was speaking an African language during the program. The television discussion was in English, so I told him that I was speaking English, and that if he actually recognized me, I was the one wearing a 'dan dogo attire. A Nigerian that I met in Grenada who had lived there for years told me when I narrated this comment to him that he was sure the person who asked the question was captivated by my dress rather than listening to my speech throughout the discussion. Could diasporic (diasporan) blacks' emotional attachment to their home continent, culture, and issues of their identity be so strong and important to them that symbols of their ancestral culture could lift them completely off the ground and even result in capturing their complete attention?

The next chapter contributes to the never-ending debate on the transatlantic slave trade. From Grenada to all countries of the Caribbean to Brazil, Mexico, the United States, Canada, England; to most countries of the New World, blacks, whether or not eager to connect to their African ancestral cultures, always acknowledge their ancestral connection to Africa. Among what differentiates the discourse of the Chinese Diaspora from the black Diaspora is the issue of slavery. Most black people in the New World were brought there as slaves, while most Chinese people perhaps fled persecution from Communist China or immigrated for economic reasons. One area of similarity, though, is the fact that many Chinese, like blacks, provided cheap labor in constructing the railway or in digging the mines in the New World. It is, therefore, not unexpected when blacks, in and outside of Africa, continue to ask questions about the transatlantic slave trade: Who was responsible? How was it organized? And from a slave descendent in the New World who is hoping to visit the homeland: How would blacks in Africa see me when I visit Africa; would they apologize to me for selling my ancestors into slavery?

All the above questions are still at the center of the several interrogations of slavery and of cultural issues among many black people, especially among those in the Diaspora. In the next chapter, I engage Henry Louis Gates (Jr.) in a dialogue about slavery and take up some of the questions that he asks in his *Wonder of the African World*. In the electronic forum of *Wonder* (which also has a print version), Gates presents amny intersesting arguments and seems to insist that every dark-skin person he encounters in some parts of Africa must be a slave; and every light-skin one, a master. How interesting is Gate's interpretations of his experiences during his travels across Africa on electronic presentations that have continued to feature in many audio-visual gadgets in the West.

Chapter 8

MIXING FICTIONS WITH FACTS, THE DEBATE ABOUT SLAVERY

〰〰

The pull for the so-called global market has been so strong in our new century that "facts" are now manufactured in "virtual factories" and real facts, the fact facts, are cast into garbage. I heard friends complained that in broad daylight, CNN called yellow green and damned innocent children or inquisitive teanager anywhere, in an Indonasian village or in a Nigerian city for example, who had thought yellow must have to mix with another substance in order to change from being yellow; that CNN fooled the otherwise smart teacher in a Brazilian classroom and through him fooled all his students, all watching the cable network! Commoditification of news has now affected how "factual" documentary is made. However sensitive an issue is, a BBC-ish scholar would not mind fabricating facts in their "virtual factories." The reinvigorated debate about slavery in the twenty-first century has taken to the fast commercial wave of the Virtual Wonders!

Who deserves an apology for trans-atlantic slave trade? Henry Louis ("Skip") Gates, in his *Wonders of the African*

World video series, makes some Africans apologize to him, thus demonstrating his belief that continental Africans need to apologize to descendants of slaves in the Diaspora. President of the Republic of Benin Mathieu Kérékou echoed a similar belief by asking for a conference where continental Africans would apologize to Diaspora Africans for slavery.[1] I'm not sure whom the president was speaking for and whether he was offering to convene such a meeting. In my view, continental and Diaspora Africans have never been enemies and have always worked together for the glory of Africa, and history is rich in examples; from Nkrumah to DuBois, Randall Robinson to Moshood Abiola. However, we do need conferences, in Africa and abroad, to reconcile our understanding of past events and to ensure that no one misrepresents the true record. Yet apology will not end the debate and misunderstandings about the transatlantic slave trade. We need to know whether Africans advertised to Europe that they were slavers and invited Europeans to buy slaves, or whether Europeans had their own plan and enticed uninformed, militarily weaker Africans to choose between "cane and carrot," to sell their own brothers and sisters. We need to know whether no African resisted the idea of his own people being sold across the ocean. We must know what happened to King Jaja of Opobo and his contemporaries[2] and whether there was truly no African resistance to the slave trade.

Now, who would apologize to continental Africans who lost their brothers and sisters to slavery, to the wife whose husband was sold away and forcefully removed to European and American plantations, to those whose cousins, aunts, and nephews were massacred and dumped in oceans for mammals to eat? Who would apologize to people whose *aso ara*, "cloths covering their bodies," were forcefully removed and left naked and their homes, nations and continent, in perpetual hunger for development? If all Africans brought to the New Worlds had remained and tilled the soil and farmed the rivers back home in their ancestral origins, Africa might be better than it is today!

In many spots in *Wonders*, Gates presents many slippery arguments to support his view that Africans practiced and still practice their own "terrible slavery." He interviews some Africans to support his views. In several instances during the interviews, Gates fails to realize that communication practically breaks down between him and his interviewees. For example, he asks one Oumar, "It [slavery] is not illegal?" Oumar responds that it is "traditional." Gates does not caution himself on whether he has gone too far in defining this specific relationship between the worker and the employer as between slave and the white slave owner in America before abolition. Some songs I heard in Nigeria that were later recounted for me perhaps shows how a Yoruba person would have interpreted what Gates calls the "slave" and "slave master" episode:

> Maso'ga di lebira Olohun,
> Gbogbo ohun ti n bami lookanje
> Ko bami so d'erin
> Koja s'ope.
>
> Gbogbo eni tin wa'se
> jeki won ri'se.
> Gbogbo eni ti o ri'se saanu funwon.
> Gbogbo nto mbami lokan je
> Ninu odun tawa yi
> je o ni'yanju.[3]

> (Oh God) don't make a master becomes a laborer
> All what makes me sad
> Let it make me laugh
> Let me be grateful (to you).
>
> All those searching for jobs,
> let them have jobs.
> All those who don't get jobs, help them.
> All what makes me sad
> This year that we are
> solve them for me (Oh God!).

Even when Oumar uses such words as *friend*, *permission*, or *payment* in the process of explaining the nature of this servitude, it does not occur to Gates to check his own preconceived view. Would anyone ever describe a slave master as, or compared him to, a slave's "friend?" Did the European slave master ever allow his slave to earn money for him/herself by taking on other employment? When did a slave master ever pay a slave for his or her labor? No, Gates is on the offensive and seems to be saying, that these people [Africans] are by nature slave hawkers, and he questions their morality for to asking for reparations from Europeans and Americans?! Well, let us examine a portion of Gates' conversation with Oumar:

> (Gates starts this portion by introducing some natives as dark-skinned slaves, and others as light-skinned masters. This was at Mopti, a market town between Bamako and Timbuktu).
>
> **Gates**: (Pointing at a native) So, he's from Timbuktu
> **Oumar**: (After inquiring from the person concerned) Timbuktu.
> **Gates**: But, how come, Oumar, how come he looks different from him?
> **Oumar**: No, he's Bella, things like that
> **Gates**: Is he a slave?
> **Oumar**: Yeah
> **Gates**: Yeah, I see. So, this man owns him?
> **Oumar**: Like that
> **Gates**: So, he's born into slavery?
> **Oumar**: Exactly. From father to son, to big father.
> **Gates**: It's not illegal?
> **Oumar**: It is traditional.
> **Gates**: Tradition.
> **Oumar**: Yeah, it's tradition.
> **Gates**: Hun. My great grand father was a slave.
> **Oumar**: Now, you, in America, is finish for that. But for this people, it is traditional.

> Every thing he have to do [that] he have to go to
> ask a friend, he have to ask him. He have to
> say do that, things like that.
> **Gates**: Does he pay him?
> **Oumar**: He pays him too.
> **Gates**: He pays him too. But this man if he wanted
> to quit and work on the river, he couldn't do
> that unless he says "yes"?
> **Oumar**: Sometimes he can say "yes", sometime
> he can say "no'.
> **Gates**: And the Bella people, no rebellion? They
> never want to fight the Tuareg?
> **Oumar**: They like it.
> **Gates**: (smiles) Yeah, they used to say that about
> Black American slaves too.[4]

No right thinking person would condone any practice anywhere that subjects anyone to socioeconomic domination, and I personally condemn any situation in Africa that makes some people lords and others serfs. However, Gates does not seem to want to examine the true situation here. He forces words into Oumar's mouth and coats the native's responses in his own biased colors. In all instances cited above, it is Gates, and not Oumar, who suggests that someone is a slave and another is a master. Oumar's level of understanding of the English language can be judged from the grammatical and phonological correctness of his responses. Oumar most likely knows the English word *slave* but chooses to use the indigenous language word for lineage or language group to describe each person he identifies for Gates in the video. Yet, in the book that accompanies the video, Gates interprets a dialogue similar to or perhaps the same as the one above with Oumar about the Tuareg and the Mella as follows:

> The man was a Tuareg, dressed in their traditional
> white gown with a bold indigo turban. With him
> was another man, very dark, dressed in an indigo
> gown, who performed all the menial tasks for the
> Tuareg tradesman. When we had passed them,
> Oumar told me that the Bella man was a slave.

> The word "slave" is not used but is the only one
> that accurately describes the traditional relation-
> ship between these two peoples. (P. 119)

Gates sounds really determined to give biased meanings to anything Oumar says. Oumar's frequent addition of
"things like that," to his responses to Gates shows that he
is not about to accept many of Gates's translations of his
speeches. I am particularly impressed that on the contrary,
Oumar answers Gates' questions only after initial confirma-
tion with those natives actually concerned.

I grew up constantly hearing a powerful Yoruba adage in
my multicultural, multiethnic Ilorin: *Eniyan l'aso* (humans
are cloths unto one another). This saying, from the repertoire
of Yoruba cultural expressions, can be very extensive; the core
meaning would be that people are there to defend each other,
to be their brothers' and sisters' keepers, and that humans are
more important to the Yoruba than money.

Basically *eniyan l'aso* is a Yoruba philosophy, which
clearly denotes that Yoruba people would rather have their
people around them than be in isolation from the people or
give away their people to others to possess. My thesis is not
to negate the theory of a willing horse in Africans or specifically among the Yorubas during the trans-atlantic slave
trade. Rather it is to establish that there is nothing inherent
in Yoruba culture that dictates that people should sell their
own people for money and materials. I would like to further
Joseph E. Inikori's opinion[5] that "conditions" were created
by Europeans for the crudest act of trading in human beings
and for transporting "captured and bought people" across the
Atlantic in the most inhuman conditions possible.

Again, I am not about to deny that Africans practiced a
kind of servitude before the European intrusion. However,
as Ali Mazrui said in his documentary, *The Africans: A Triple
Heritage*, the degree of callousness of the European enslave-
ment of Africans was unknown to Africans. Let me go once
again to Yoruba rhetoric: *Eni to l'eru lo l'eru, eni leru lo l'eru*
(To whomever belongs the "slave," belongs the slave's prop-

erties, and whomever has slave's properties has the "slave"). *T'aa ba ran ni ni'se eru afi t'omo jee* (When a person is sent on an errand that portrays him/her as a "slave," he or she should deliver it as a freeborn). It is not yet the time or the place to analyze every phonemic, morphological, and syntactic structure of these Yoruba adages; neither do I need now explain their sociocultural meanings. What is crucial for the purpose of this discussion is that Yoruba has a word, *eru*, often wrongly translated as equivalent to the English word "slave" by many contemproary Yoruba scholars. As Toyin Falola once said, *eru* is not always the same as "slave,"[6] neither is a Yoruba person referring to *eru mi*, "my eru," the same as an American white slave owner referring to "my slave." *O s'eru sinmi* means "He/she served me," *O s'eru sinle baba re*, "He/she served his/her country; as in the case of the one-year national youth service program in Nigeria; *eru Anabi*, follower of Anabi (Falola). The question we must ask is whether the Yoruba culture at any time saw *eru* as less human, i.e., as black slaves were treated in Europe. Since historians have repeatedly reminded us that Europeans practiced slavery on their own before they enslaved Africans. We may also want to ask: Did Europeans treat European slaves as less human as they treated black slaves? Did any non-European create any "condition" for Europeans to be shipped abroad? How many of them were massacred as blacks were? How many were thrown into the Atlantic Ocean, beheaded like chickens! Where on earth were European slaves taken and maltreated to such devastating degrees as blacks were?!

The philosophy of *eniyan (enia) l'aso* would prove that Africans (or Yoruba people) who captured opponents during interethnic wars used them to boost their own population. Some powerful warriors married female captors, and other captors served their masters in various economic and cultural capacities. Without doubt, this attitude was terrible and degrading of their fellow human beings, but it is far less callous than the European slavers' subjugation of Africans. African practice of servitude is not reason enough to initiate or to justify the transatlantic slave trade. The farms worked, and the economies developed by the indigenous African labor were Africa's. Descendants of hitherto laborers have become political leaders in many parts of Africa. If our searchlights are sharp enough we will find among contemporary African presidents some whose foreparents were domestic farm workers.

When Africans practiced indigenous servitude, I'm not sure the African master had manufactured chains and padlocks to further dehumanize fellow Africans. Part of the "conditions" Europeans created for the transatlantic slave trade was the importation of chains, padlocks, guns, and various crude gadgets to Africa and the obvious demonstration of their uses to the Africans. If what we read about how Europeans beat and exiled King Jaja of Opobo were true, if the story about how they subjugated the proud kingdom of the Benin people waere anything to learn from, Africans had to cooperate when Europeans came to them with carrots, asking to ship away fellow Africans; for after carrots would have come heavy canes.

Let us take a brief time to peruse this Yoruba anecdote: *O nwa owo lo, o waa pade iyi l'ona. Bi o ba ri owo ohun kini iwo yo fira?* (You set off on a journey in search of money, and right on your way, you met prestige/honor. If you had eventually got the money what would you have purchased with it?) I am not so sure that the Yoruba people, and indeed Africans, had particular yearnings for materials such that they would be all out to sell their own people for devastation. Of course, some African leaders—the Sesessekos, the Abachas, and the Babangidas, formerly dictators of their respective African countries—of this "neocolonial" generation proved particularly carnivorous in their treatement of fellow Africans and behaved as if they had not been brought up with traditional African ethics. The African oral tradition, for example, i.e., the Yoruba adage *oruko rere osan ju wura ati fadaka lo* (a good name is better than gold and silver), shows that prestige, and honor were preoccupations greater to them than money, and honor came when they were generous to their own people, when they spent for their people's welfare, and served them selflessly, not when they sold their brothers and sisters to the highest bidder.

SLAVERY AND THE AFRICAN KINGS

Yes, let's turn one of the Yoruba adages I cited in this text upside down (isn't the issue at stake itself upside down?): *Won ran Oba n'ise eru, Oba je'se bi eru,* (The King was sent a message as a slave, he delivered it as a slave). Yes, African kings and chiefs were slaves in the hands of the white slavery mongers. As Wole Soyinka suggested in his "Intervention,"[7] we should not sympathize with the African king-collaborator. We should not speculate either about what could have happened to them had they refused to collaborate with the slavers. Yes, the kings should have resisted, and history would have judged them brave warriors? How has history judged King Jaja of Opobo, who said "to hell" with the slavers and the colonialists? How does it judge the Benin king, the chiefs, and the masses who insisted that the British must respect their culture and protocol? Yet, the same history and historians today say they deserve no reparations! Did the Europeans enslave King Jaja and the king of Benin, or did they leave them in their kingly robes? How can we understand what informed those kings' choices for resistance? How sincere are we when we hail or condemn African kings and chiefs either way? Has whatever decision they made nullify the genocide of the tranatlantic slave trade? Can we discuss the transatlantic slave trade outside racial reasons?

Would it be wrong to say that racism (the belief that blacks are subhuman) was at the root of how Europeans prosecuted the trade?

In Ali Mazrui's submission,[8] he makes references to a respected Nigerian historian's assertion that African Chiefs were forced into the transatlantic slave trade. Mazrui's lines are interesting:

The formulation is mine, but the logic is what professor Ajayi has brought into the debate. African Chiefs were BLACKMAILED (or WHITE-MAILED) into becoming slavers for the white man. Since the Trans-Atlantic slave trade was DEMAND- DRIVEN, and the demand was in the West, Africans were forced into collaboration. Often literally at the point of a gun.

The "carrot-or-cane" policy of white slavers cannot be dismissed with a wave of the hand whenever Africans' participation in transatlantic slave trade is discussed. Yet, I might be among the first to agree that African Chiefs should have chosen to receive the white man's cane and resisted him to the last. But, would it be the kings alone that would have been maimed and or put into slavery? Perhaps the entire continent and the black race would have been forced into captivity. No, no speculation.

I think history has proven that a choice to resist European domination may be practicable in African-European dealings in the twenty-first century—despite neocolonialism and global trade exploitation. It could have been suicidal for Africans to dare the white man even before the mid-twentieth century. I need not repeat the many examples that we already know, and really, I don't want to speculate!

It seems to me that Africans compete well, sometimes even imitate the white man in many areas, but have refused to degenerate to the level of callousness of the white executors of the transatlantic slave trade.

I am often amused to hear the Yoruba adage, *B'Oyinbo mu tii maa m'ekoogbona. Omi gbona kan naa lajo n mu* [If the white man drinks tea, I'll drink *ekoogbona*—hot corn-drink (after all, we both drink hot water/liquid!)] It is with this popular saying that I would like to return to my previous discussion on the terminology used for the English word *slave* in some African languages, especially the Yoruba language. The *eru* (there's another word: *iwofa*) tradition among the Yoruba is basically a tradition of servitude. An *eru* is simply a servant. Perhaps "serf" is far better a translation of *eru* than slave: *Eru Oba*, the king's servant. Yoruba people can compete so well with Europeans and can easily locate equivalent cultural elements from their locality, as shown in the Ilorin Yoruba humorous adage quoted above. However, never have the Yoruba people, and indeed no African culture to my knowledge, ever even thought of, let alone actually competed with, the brutish British and American slavery traditions. Although there was, and still is, *ekoogbona* for the tea the English presented to them, never have Africans practiced such a debasement of humanity as slavery. There is no word, with apology to the Whorfians,[2] in the thoughts of the Yoruba people (Africans) for slavery!

Among the Hausa people, the Yoruba's neighbors spread in many areas of West Africa, modern writers often use *bawa* or *baiwa* for "slave." Like *eru*, *bawa* simply means "servant," not "slave." Many contemporary Hausa scholars have used *bauta* for slavery. However, *bauta* in Hausa *gangariya*, deep-rooted Hausa, is worship or service, and many will say, *na bautawa Allah*, "I worshipped God." *Na bauta wa sarki*, "I served the king!" *Na bauta maka* can even be extended to mean "I served/respected you." Perhaps *eru oba* will be the same as *dogarin sarkin* in Hausa, or *bawan sarki* (meaning, the king's servant). Because of the importance of the "service" meaning of the word *bawa*, many Hausa people today answer to the name Bawa. I don't think any person would like to be called "slave" in terms of the transatlantic slave trade. Even Uncle Toms wouldn't use "Slave" as a first name, however happy they are with their masters. Cato, Dr. Gaines's house slave in *The Escape; or A Leap for Freedom* (1858) by William Wells Brown, proved at the end of the day that he would raher answer to a name of freedom.

My American students are forever asking me why Elesin Oba, the king's horseman in Wole Soyinka's *Death and the King's Horseman* (1975), was treated with reverence and cultural dignity, when, in fact, he was only a servant, an *eru*, to the king and was meant to "die" because the king "died." I always reply that Elesin Oba was not a slave, that as a servant of the king and the community, he did not, at any time, lose his status as a human being; and that an Elesin actually won greater glory by the sheer importance of the service of saving human lives and ensuring community harmony by "committing death"[10] to accompany the kabiyesi, king. As Olori Elesin, leader of all the king's Horsemen, his position attracted more honor to him. Certainly no Elesin Oba would ever cease to be regarded as a human being, even if he is terribly disadvantaged in any situation.

Anyone who still hasn't got the idea that race made the big difference in the execution of the transatlantic slave trade should read Soyinka's poem "Telephone Conversation" as evidence of a not too distant past. And I'd be taken aback if he or she continues to limit his/her polemics to demeaning the African chiefs instead of understanding their predicament. The European slavers did not see Africans as human beings. The darkness of Africans' skins was what, to them, defined Africans, not the lightness of Africans' palms. Nonetheless, if the argument for reparation is based on racism alone, it would still be a genuine one. The French in overpowering the English dined with the English, encouraged their own princes and princesses to marry British princes and princesses; the Romans did not chain the Greeks to trees or pack them like sardines, shopping them across oceans and seas. However, the European slavers considered that subdued Africans weren't human beings, thus they justified perpetuating anything and everything evil upon them.

Yes, we need more studies into the kinds of *eru* traditions in Africa. We need metalanguage scholars (the Awobuluyis, the Bamgboses, and the Dalhatu Muhammads in Nigeria) to find equivalents for some foreign words. My point here is that while it is crucial to continue to interrogate the issue of slavery and all the atrocities committed by Africans and non-Africans alike regarding the transatlantic slave trade, it is important to understand deeply rooted African traditions from different African ethnic and cultural perspectives as we judge African involvement in the transatlantic slave trade. It is important to make clear that not every black person from the Diaspora goes to Africa like Henry Louis Gates and blames Africans and demands apology from them. W.E.B. Dubois took Ghanaian citizenship and died in Ghana, and he was only one of several examples of black cultural and intellectual leaders who understood the complexity of the so-called African involvement in slavery rather than travel around the continent in search of apology. Similarly, Mathieu Kérékou's offer of apology to the African Americans has taken some of his ministers to different black communities in the USA. While the interaction that ensued from such a venture is mutually beneficial, it is certain that not every African American waits for an African head of state to send them a party of apologizing diplomats. Whether in the Caribbean, the United States, Africa, or anywhere else in the world having a substantial black population, the questions of cultural survival and historical grounding seem to be of a higher order.

Chapter 9

WAKA: THE DIALECTICAL ESSENCE OF AN ILORIN ISLAMIC ORAL POETRY

❦

The development of Ilorin multiculturalism and pluralism is a very interesting one. It started as multiculturalism of ethnic groups and of religions. Today, it has remained a multiculturalism of ethnic groups with Islam as the dominant religion of the Ilorin people. In many ways, the development of *waka* as an Ilorin traditional genre and as an important symbol of Ilorin multiculturalism reflects the community's history and social life. The Ilorin *waka*, even though delivered mainly in Yoruba language, carries Hausa and Fulani cultural flavors with Islamic social contents. From approximately the sixteenth century to the early eiteenth century, Muslim immigrants from Hausa, Fulani, Gobir, and Mali ethnic nations settled in Ilorin. As these immigrants were mainly Muslims, Islamic religion was gradually introduced to other Ilorin people.[1] Finally in A.D. 1823, an Islamic dynasty was establihed and it became the official religion of Ilorin. Yoruba traditional religions of Oya, Ifa, Obatala, Egungun, Igunnun, idol worshipping, and by implication, their poetic forms, were officially outlawed. It was about this time that *waka* was introduced.

It is clear from discoveries in research on Waka that the *waka* artist does not only sing in praise of the Prophet Muhammed and teach Islamic religious rites to its local audience,[2] he or she, and very substantially too, addresses the perpetual injustice between human beings and human beings in the society, critizes the excesses of political ambition and power mongering, and even calls for progressive changes on the socioeconomic situations of the community. In this chapter, I trace the development and performance techniques of *waka* and to highlight what I call the dialectical essence of the poetic form. By dialectical essence I mean both the ethnic or cultural flavor of it and how it serves as an agent of change in the society in terms of dialical mterialism.

NAME AND DEVELOPMENT OF *WAKA*

Waka is a Hausa word for songs of any kind. Although Ilorin *waka* art takes its name after this Hausa word, it means a specific kind of Islamic oral genre in Ilorin. In fact, the articulation of the word in Ilorin is different from that of its protoform. Yoruba linguistlc peculiarity has influenced the Ilorin phonetic version of the word. The Hausa word for song has a vowel length - /aa/ - after the bilabial approximant /W/. Hausa has different types of the voiceless velar consonant /K/. Apart from the /K/, which is the same as the one in Yoruba, one of the other types available to a Hausa speaker is the labialized velar /Kʷ/, the glottalized labio-velar /kʷ/, the palatalized velar /kȷ/, and the glotalized velar /k'/. The last one here /'/ is the consonant realized in the Hausa word for songs. The last vowel of the word - /a/ - is a short vowel. So, the word for songs in Hausa is phonemically transcribed /waak'a/. Though the vowel length is not ususally marked in the Hausa Roman script, it is always realized in *Ajami* writing system.[3]

124

However, the word for this Ilorin Islamic oral genre is *waka*, phenemically transcribed /waka/ with two short /a/ vowels and with a simple voiceless velar consonant /k/. *Waka* art, therefore, is an interesting symbol of multiculrualism among Ilorin people: Hausa, Yoruba, and Islam, and all melt into a uniquely Ilorin traditional form!

Waka (at a smaller, part-time scale) started in Ilorin ever before the establishment of the Ilorin Emirate in A.D. 1823.[4] During public preachings, the *alfas* (Islamic scholars and preachers) composed Hausa and Yoruba Islamic oral songs to ensure a successful tranmission of their message to the people. This was in line with the general practice in the whole of the Sokoto Caliphate where, according to Shehu Umar Abdullahi,[5] Islamic songs were composed and were chanted during public preachings. This oral form, *orin esin*[6] or *orin waasi*, is the mother of *waka*. These songs, sung by the Hausa jihadist-immigrants in Ilorin, simply called /waaka/, were well received by the people. At this period, there was a massive propagation of Islam. The Ilorin people were encouraged to abandon all non-Islamic ceremonies and songs like *Egungun* and *Igunnu* festivals and chants. The Islamic mode of celebration was therefore introduced instead. So, the present mode of *waka*, born out of *orin esin*, was later developed and first performed during ceremonies marking the completion of the learning of every *yis-hi* (chapters) of the Holy Qur'an, and later performed at the grand finale, after the completion of the whole sixty chapters of the Qur'an. These celebrations, whose grand finale performance is similar to what Finnegan[7] describes as an initiation into adulthood in some African cominunities, is called *wolimat*, an Arabic word for "celebration" or "ceremony." In other words, the final *wolimat* is usually marked as a part of marriage activities of the new adult. In the first stage of its development, it was the Qur'anic school pupils and their *alfa*, "teacher," taking a clue from what they saw and heard from *orin esin* that rendered the *wolima waka*. After the completion of every *yis-hi* of the Qur'an, they went round the town singing the glory of God, praising the Prophet of Islam, Muhammad, and expressing the gratitude of the celebrants to their parents, who sent them to the Qur'anic schools. They also mocked those pupils who could not come to such schools. The following was among the songs rendered:

> Eyin tee kewu, ekuuya
> Awa n jaye kalamu
> Ina'l hakku nasiira,
> Wa akali a dada[8]

> You who do not seek Qur'anic knowledge we pity you on your suffering
> We are enjoying (our world) from the *Kalam*-pen
> Definitely truth shall prevail over falsehood!

Later, when the pupils started graduating from the Qur'anic schools (usually after learning Qur'anic recitation, translation, and some other Islamic religious books) and were ready for marriage, the pupils and their *alfa* organized what I call the *Grand Finale wolimat* for him/her and sang the *waka*. This was done both on the eve of the *wolimat* day (especially by the *waka* Group as shall be explained later) and on the *wolimat* day when the bride or bridegroom (as the case might be) was expected to read from the first two chapters of the Holy Qur'an for friends, relatives, and well-wishers who would then present the celebrants with monetary and material gifts. Gift presentations in honor of celebrants are totally different from the gift offerings to *waka* artists (more on this later).

It can be said therefore that, propelled by the material rewards of *waka* performance, many *alfas* learned in Islamic theology took an interest in it and started the full-time practice and development of *waka* art, perhaps as early as around A.D. 1830[9] Thus *waka* became well institutionalised in Ilorin and has continued to the twenty-first century. People not taking part in *wolimat* and during other social celebrations in Ilorin also chant *waka* songs performed during *wolimat*.

TYPES AND PERFORMANCE TECHNIQUES OF ILORIN *WAKA*

There are three types of Ilorin *waka*. The first type, the Group *waka* art, is the mother *waka*! The other two types derive their performance songs from the first. The Group *waka* is made up of a group of professional *waka* artists and a *Waka* lead singer. They often perform on the eve of *wolimat* to entertain *wolimat* celebrants and their guests. They help to psychologically prepare the *wolimat* man or woman for the task of Qur'anic recitation test that is ahead of him or her the following morning. *Wolimat* here means *wolimat Qur'an*, where the person who has successfully completed learning to recite the entire Qur'an would perform graduation rites and ceremonies on a Wednesday. This ceremony is often done as part of wedding rites in Ilorin. It ushers in the week-long traditional Ilorin wedding that begins after the *wolimat* eve on Tuesday night.

The Group *waka* artists are also invited to thanksgiving ceremonies and to turbaning ceremony. The lead singer also performs alone on batle fronts, encouraging soldiers and assuring them of success. They are well rewarded with money and materials either during *wolimat* or battle front performances. When they perform during *wolimat* people troop out to present them with money and material gifts, and the *wolimat* lead singer makes sure he or she recognizes the gift by publicly announcing the names of the benefactor. *Owo Alhaja Sifawu re oo!* (Here is the money gift from Alhaja Sifawu!) The *waka* artists then sing prayers for and shower gratitude on the benefactor and then acknowledge the next one. According to Labeka,[10] the king of *waka*, his grandfather, Ilyasu Malarabuka, was offered slaves and horses for a successful performance during the Ilorin-Offa war. In contemporary times, the Group *Waka* is also invited to other public engagements like lunches and public motivation activities. *Waka* artists of this type, especially the lead singer are usually versed in the Qur'an and the Hadith (sayings of

Prophet Muhammad). To become a traditional Group *Waka* artist, one has to be apprenticed under an established *waka* lead singer for as long as eight to ten years or even more. Labeka was on apprenticeship under the famous *waka* artist Dodo for twenty years. To be qualified for an apprenticeship, one must not only be versed in the Qur'an and the Hadith, he or she must be of good character, must have good voice and must be physically fit. It must be mentioned that the twenty-first century has brought about what I will described as an electronic age Group *Waka*, led by much younger Ilorin persons, who are talented singers, often with knowledge of Qur'an and Hadith (although this is no longer a strict requirement), but often with access to recording studios to make records that are then widely sold. Although *waka* groups have been initiated into record making since the late seventies, as the Alhaji Wahab (Oorelope)-led *Waka* Group, and other quite popular *waka* audio records, would also show in Ilorin to the late 1980s, the twenty-first century electronic *waka* are audio-visual, often on VCDs and distributed nationally and internationally. Contemporary *waka* groups now post their records and video performances on YouTube available for download around the world. The advent of global century *waka* shows the strong influence of our global electronic technology on deeply cultural traditions of Ilorin! As an Ilorin person living abroad in the United States, access to these electronic *waka* has been important in maintaining the cultural attachment of my, in American parlace, immediate family to our indigenous home.

Among past successful professional *waka* artists in Ilorin were Ilyasu Malarabuka in Idiape, Maluma Agbarere, Abdul-Rahman Oba-Waka, Ajisodun Adangba, Dodo Alore, Aadi Oke Apomu and Amosa Jogbo-jogbo. Both AbdulRahman and Dodo rose to become kings of *waka*, *Oba Waka*, during their respective periods. Other professional *waka* artists at the turn of the twenty-first century included Labeka (of blessed memory), who was also turbaned by the Emir of Ilorin, Muhammad Zulkarneini Ganbari, as *Oba-Waka*. Others are Olohungbebe Ladipo, Adelope Pakata, Alhaji Amada, Alfa

Laaro, Isa Olorin Agbaji, Abdul Ita-Egba, Alhaji Adebimpe, and Alhaji Mayaki. There are also Atinuke Ojuekun, Ralia Bada, and Ruka Batimoluwasi Sulemana. Because of the strict apprenticeship requirements of the profession of *waka*, very few people went into the professional *waka* art in Ilorin within the traditional circles. For example, in 1990, there were forty-five *waka* groups in the entire Ilorin Emirate.[11] Consequently, especially during the peak days of performance for any of the traditional *waka* groups listed above, one Group *waka* was usually booked for six to seven places on a single *wolimat* night. They might even have spent as little as one hour in every performance and then moved on to another venue until they completed the round. The ages of *waka* performers were within forty and seventy-five years.

The second type of Ilorin *waka* is the one-man *waka*.[12] Here, individual freelance *waka* artists go around the town chanting the praises of the Prophet Muhammed and praying for the public. These freelance poets, whose acctities are very similar to Almajiri pupils, wonder around in nooks and corners of Ilorin. These set of *waka* artists do not require any professional training.

In addition, it is not required that these freelance poets have any deep knowledge of the Qur'an, eventhough few of them are really well-versed. They attend ceremonies, whether or not invited. They also move through the sreets, often from one house to the other, at the very early hours of the morning (usually after the early morning prayers), in the afternoon, and in the evening. They stay in corridors, stand in the passageway, or in front of their targets (often people they would like to sing for in order to obtain favors from them) and sing for them. The most popular artist of this *waka* type in Ilorin was Baba Gani Eto, who performed in the Okekura area. Other one-man *waka* artists include AlhaJi Salako, AlhaJi Suleiman, Ayinla and Suleman Salahu. Their ages range between forty and eighty.

The third type is the Housewives *Waka*.[13] Though performed on a group basis, most Housewives' *Waka* have no standing or permanent groups or group members. They usually perform during traditional Ilorin ceremonies like wedding, naming, and thanksgiving celebration and during funeral services for quite elderly people whose death is seen as caused by old age. The housewives just get themselves together, often spontaneously, and sing, moving around to perform for the deceased, for the bereaved and his or her relatives and other guests attending the event.

The modes of performances of all the three types of Ilorln *waka* art are very simple. The *waka* artists, like the Dadakuada and Baalu artists, perform by improvization. The question of occasional rehearsal or practice as we have in a few modern-day traditional oral arts—like Dadakuada and Hausa oral songs—is totally irrelevant in *waka*. However, the style and pattern of Ilorin *waka*, true to Parry/Lord's oral formulaic theory,[14] is a carryover from generation to generation. It is fixed in the minds of the performers and their audience. There are some differences in the mode of delivery of the various types of Ilorin *waka*: The Group *Waka* art, as its name suggests, is performed in groups. Every group, as I have said before, has a leader whose name the group bears. So, every group is made up a lead singer and the chorus subgroup. The chorus is usually made up of about twenty members. The group normally starts performing around eleven o'clock at night in the *wolimat* eve. They perform in open field within the compound of the celebrant. All members of the chorus subgroup sit on a mat or a number of mats. The lead singer sits on a chair. The performance usually has an opening, a middle, and a closing. The lead artist starts by rendering prayers to Allah, asking Him to bless the gathering, and then declaring the commencement of his art in God's name. The following is an example of an opening *waka* song:

Lead singer:	Ahuzu billahi mina shaitani Rajeem,
	Bismillahi, Rahmani, Raheem,
	Oba olola, sati Ramani,
	Waa pelu wa, Oba Olohun,
	Laa ilaa ha.
Chorus:	Ila llahu.

130

Lead singer: Gabasi la koju si yi, Yaa Rahmanu
Ma sai saanu wa, Rabbi Olohun.
Laa ilaa ha
Chorus: Ila llahu.
Lead singer: Eni to ba ti gun oke arafa lo lee
fenunso
Oba alansu ni oluwa mi
Pelu iya iyawo
Pelu gbogbo awon aalabase
Laa ilaa ha
Chorus: Ila llahu.[15]

Lead singer: I seek refuge against the devil,
the accursed
I start with the name of Allah, the
Beneficent, the Merciful
The Royal King, the Beneficent
ruler, please assist us
There is no god worthy of worship.
Chorus: Except Allah.
Lead singer: We're facing the *Gabas* oh you the
Beneficent
Do please bless us my Lord, Our
Lord,
Here is no god worthy of worship.
Chorus: Except Allah.
Lead singer: He who has climbed mountain
Arafat, can explain in detail
My Lord is a sympathetic King
Do please support the father of
the bride
Do please support the mother of
the bride
There is no god worthy of worship.
Chorus: Except Allah.

As is typical of Muslims, the *waka* poets start by seeking refuge against Satan, the devil, who is believed to be capable of misleading everyone and of bringing confusion and mis-understanding among the people in the performance venue.

Also in this opening song, the *waka* poets showered encomiums on God. He is described from His popular ninety-nine names as Beneficent and Merciful.[16] The following statement further glorifies Allah: "'There is no god worthy of worship except Allah." Both the lead singer and the chorus sometimes sing this simultaneously at the end of the chanting stanzas. The statement revolves around the concept of Unity of God in Islam.[17] The poets ask God to bless them, saying: "My Lord, Our Lord." In other words, they seek spiritual and material gifts from Allah. Various material gifts, which the celebrant and his or her relatives and guests would give them, are definitely part of what the *waka* artists count as blessings from God.

After the opening, the performance then moves to the middle stage. Here, the *waka* artists praise and pray for people who offer them money or sometimes clothes. Normally, all money spent here is seen as *sadakah* (Islamic alms) by the audience. Such gifts are supposed to aid the acceptance of all prayers rendered by the *waka* artists for the patron or patroness, his or her parents, deceased relatives, and for members of the audience. So, the money or material gifts made here is taking the place of the sacrificial goat, which is traditionally killed to aid the acceptance of prayers by God. It is an archetypal pattern of what Bayo Ogunjimi would call "petting God, the spoilt child" to win His favors.[18] The following songs[19] are thus rendered:

Lead singer: Owo Salamatu ree o, ore Iyawo,
Ofun min legbe ee wa
Oni kin sadua fun iyawo ati oko iyawo
Oni Olohun yio fun 'yawo lomo olore
Ya Jalla Jallaluhu,
Oluwa Dakun bun 'yawo lokunrin.
Bun yawo lobinrin
Bun yawo lomo to yayi bi Annabi Yusufu.

Chorus: Bun yawo lokunrin, bunyawo lobinrin.

Lead singer: Ani o bun la finju bi Annabi
Yusufu.

Chorus: Bun yawo lokunrin, bun yawo
lobinrin.

Lead singer: Bun yawo lolowo, bun yawo lolola.
Bun yawo lo ni oye bi Sulaymana.

Chorus: Bun yawo lokunrin, bun yawo
lobinrin.

Lead singer: Bun yawo larewa bi Nana Fati-
matu.

Chorus: Bun yawo lokunrin, bun yawo
lobinrin.

Lead singer: This is the money gift from
Salamatu.
The friend of the bride
She gave me ten fives
She said I should pray for the
bride and
the bridegroom.
She pleaded with God to give the
bride
a good child
Oh You Almighty, the Mightiness
Please give the bride male child
Give the bride female child
Give the child a handsome child
like Prophet Yusuf.

Chorus: Give the bride female child,
Give the child male child.

Lead singer: Give the bride a neat child like
Prophet Yusuf.

Chorus: Give the bride male child, give the
bride male child, give the bride
female child.

Lead singer: I said give the bride a fashionable
child, like Prophet Yusuf.

Chorus: Give the bride male child, give the
bride female child.

Lead singer: Give the bride rich child, blessed
child, high positioned child, like
Prophet Sulaiman.

133

Chorus:	Give the bride male child, give the bride female child.
Lead singer:	Give the bride beautiful child like our mother, Fatimata.
Chorus:	Give the bride male child, give the bride female child.

The *waka* singers pray to God to bless the bride with fine, respected, successful, and responsible children like the various prophets of Allah and like the great Muslim personalities whose stories are told in the Qur'an and Islamic historical books. In this case, the patron often also comes out and asks for prayers from the *waka* artists. The lead-singer prays, most especially, for a successful *wolimat* ritual for the celebrant in the *wolimat* day. It is believed that a celebrant could develop cold feet on the wolimat day and could find it difficult to recite the Qur'an. Some people believe that the bride or bridegroom could fall sick or even die on the *wolimat* day. So, the *waka* artists pray vigorously for a peaceful and successful performance of *wolimat* ritual by the patron on the day following the eve. It seems to me that part of the importance of this *wolimat* eve *waka* performance is to prepare psychologically and through performance prayers for the *wolimat*.

Also, during this middle stage of the performance, the lead artist tells stories of great religious leaders and prophets and encourages people to imitate them. The artist also attacks the ills (social, political, and economic) in the society and calls for a change of behavior of society for better. It is also at this stage that the singer adopts various performance patterns, changing from one technique to the other. Apart from the call and response or Lead-and-chorus techniques that the performers often use in *waka*, the *waka* singers also adopt what can be called a speech-giving technique and the chanting-session' technique. In the speech-giving technique, the lead singer stops singing and resorts to real talking, narrating and speech making. Such talk is sometimes done at the highest pitch of the performer's voice. For example, the performer may be addressing issues that relate to social, economic, and political rots of society, and he or she may be adopting some Islamic stories intended to give more force and concreteness to his stand on such issues. When this technique is adopted, the chorus is usually cut out; but the audience listens, paying rapt attention to the proceedings. This is perhaps the most important demonstration of the respect that the audience has for *waka*, as the audience listens to the *waka* artists and actually quotes widely from such speeches later in the community. The chanting-session technique is similar to the techniques adopted by the Ijala chanters and the Almajiri chanters. When the chanting-session technique is adopted by the lead singer, only he or she chants.

The following are two or three examples of *waka* rendered in some of the techniques just discussed:

a. *Speech-giving technique.*

Labeka:

> Allahu Akbar! Tee yan baro wipe Olohun
> oni bi ohun, iro ni. Ati olowo atolola,
> atolori - olori ile, olori ijo, olori ilu,
> Agbara ti en lo lati fi ni jamaa lara! Lo ni,
> ta lo lese bi Sayyidina Abubakar?
> Mo bere ni'! Ati olori, ati mekunnun?
> Abubakar sejoba pelu iberu Olohun.[20]

Labeka:

> Allah is the Greatest! If a person thinks that God will not demand for explanations from him or her, the person must be kidding!
> The rich, the royal, the leader-the leader of a family, leader of an association, leader of a town-the power you use to make life difficult for people
> Today, tell me, who can do like Caliph Abubakar? I ask you!
> Among the leaders and the led poor people! Abubakar led with the fear of God. (my translation)

135

b. *Chanting-session technique.*

Ruka: Owo Alaja wa Aduke.

> Iyale iyawo
> Ee ni ri nti n ba ninnuje
> Iyale iyawo je nun re o dun un,
> Olohun mafoju ta Aduke ati n tobani
> Owo Alhaja wa Rabi
> Awon naa mo wo paun meji abo wa,
> Olohun ko mo da mun re Rabi
> Olohun komo doti re Rabi
>
> Ee ba n pe Olohun ko man yeye re Rabi
> Olohun wo ta saju eda ti mo le man ran
> Eku inawo ojo fun Rukayyatu
> Ooba to tobi, mori poun marun gbaa
> Olohun-Oba dakun ma se emin eyin
> jabute
> Olohun wo ta saju eda ti mo le maran
> Tori asaju eda tinje Muhammad o.[21]

Ruka: The money gift from our Alhaja Aduke

> The senior to the bride
> You will not be touched by sadness
> Senior-to-the-bride.
> Let her be happy, oh God!
> Please God don't disgrace Aduke and her
> belongings!
> The money gift from our Alhaja Rabi
> She also brought money-gift of five-naira
> May God not trouble you, Rabi
> May God not make you dirty, Rabi.
>
> Please (audience) say on my behalf that
> God will not make you useless, Rabi
> Oh God (do these) because of the leader of
> Mankind that I include in my talk,
> Thanks much for the gifts the other day, for

Rukayyatu
May the Mighty God not spend you with
the time
May He pleased not shorten your life
Oh God, (do this) because of the leader
of mankind
that I include in my talk!

Please anyone who knows God should
say amen!

c. *Lead-and-chorus technique.*

Lead singer: Jeko dara f'aji Amedi Alakoso o o
Olohun je o dara faji Amedi
Alakoso
Apada si aburu so won pelu e
Je o dara faji Amedi Alakoso.

Chorus: Amin, je o dara faji Amedi
Aiakoso o
Je o dara faji Amedi Alakoso
Apada s' aburu so won pelu e
Je o dara faji Ahmedi Alakoso.

Lead-singer: Alakoso ko ni foju tio, Aji Amedi

Chorus: Amin, Amin, je o dara faji Amedi
Alakoso

Lead singer: Je o dara faji Ahmedi Alakoso
Ani Olohun ya Rabbana, komaa
te o ri.

Chorus: Amin, amin, je o dara faji Amedi
Alakoso.[22]

Lead singer: Let it be good for Aii Amedi
Alakoso
Oh God, let it be good for Aji
Amedi Alakoso
A change-for-worse, do save him
from
Let it be good for Aji Amedi
Alakoso.

Chorus:	Amin, let it be good for Aji Amedi Alakoso
	Let it be good for Aji Amedi Alakoso
	A chasge-for-worse, do sate him from it
	Let it be good for Aji Amedi Alakoso.
Lead singer:	Alakoso, life will not shame you, Aji Amedi
Chorus:	Amen, amen, let it be good for Aji Amedi Alakoso
Lead singer:	I said Oh God our Lord, should not supress your fame.
Chorus:	Amen, amen, let it be good for Aji Amedi Alakoso.

The lead singer may introduce any pattern or technique he or she likes at any time, choosing from the three patterns used in Group *Waka* performance. When the performance reaches its climax, the lead singer gets up to dance. As he or she chants, the lead singer gesticulates and invites the chorus and the audience to partiipate. The members of the chorus group and the audience usually become very involved in the performance at this moment and thus the response is spontaneous. Every *waka* artist is seen moving his or her head and other parts of his or her body in a gentle dance to the rhythm of the *waka* songs.

The closing of the Group *Waka* performance is done by praying for the fans and thanking everybody for their generous gifts. Allah is also praised for making the day successful. At this stage the chorus group comes out to do what can be described as a round-up dance. These members twist their buttocks and dance up and down. The members of the audience who have been active participants also join in by clapping for the artists, hailing the performance, offering more gifts, dancing themselves, and generally responding with the ovation, *Eyonbo onse Olohun! Salallahu alayhi wassalam!* At this moment, the performers are in ecstasy. People are on their feet to see the dancing. Some members of the chorus group also continue the rhythmic movement of parts of their bodies while seated. They also provide drumlike rhythmic sounds orally. They become highly involved here, and in some instances it is only one of them that serve as what can be described as Iyaalu drummer by mouth, the lead drummer. He jacks, brakes, and controls the dancing steps of the dancers (all through sounds from his mouth). Such an onomatopoeic rhythmic rendition brings the performance to its climax, leading to the actual finale of performance. The following is an excerpt from Ruka Suleimana's performance at this stage:

Ruka:	E pe 'seli' ara min.
Chorus:	Sali ala Muhammad.
Ruka:	E pe 'seli' ara min.
Chorus:	Sali ala Muhamma.
Ruka:	Muhammadaa.
Chorus:	Sali ala Muhammad.
Ruka:	E pe Muhammaduu.
Chorus:	Sali ala Muhamma.
Ruka:	Ike Oluwa.
Chorus:	Sali ala Muhamma.
Ruka:	Atiola Oluwa.
Chorus:	Sali ala Muhamma.
Ruka:	Ko ma b.a titilola.
Chorus:	Sali ala Muhaxma.[23]

Ruka:	Say, peace, my people.
Chorus:	Peace be unto Muhamma.
Ruka:	Say, peace, my people.
Chorus:	Peace be unto Muhamma.
Ruka:	Muhammadaa.
Chorus:	Peace be unto Muhammad.
Ruka:	Say Muhammadu.
Chorus:	Peace be unto Muhammad.
Ruka:	The blessings of God.
Chorus:	Peace be unto Muhammad.
Ruka:	And the Mercies o! God.
Chorus:	Peace be unto Muhammad.

Ruka: Unto the eternal blessing.
Chorus: Peace be unto Muhammad.

Repetitions, metaphors, similes, and other artistic tools are employed. The lead singer says further in the songs that when it comes to dancing, she is an insect. She dances with her back like a snail or a hen. Dancing makes her so happy that she prefers it to eating food; as long as the dancing is in adoration of Prophet Muhammad. And so the lead artist joins the dance. Some members of the audience may also join in. Others clap, hail, and jump in appreciation of the performance. It is when the ovation is loudest that the performance suddenly stops and the performers get up and leave.

The one-man *waka* artist, on the other hand, goes on his performance alone. His main performance technique is the Chanting-session technique. He goes from house to house, ceremony or to ceremony. Many people, especially children, gather around him to listen. They applaud good performances with claps and shouts of "heeee" and with monetary gifts. The artist also does his individual dancing. Anyone among the members of the audience can join him in dancing. People often do so when the one-man *waka* performance is at its performance climax.

The Housewives *waka* art, as the name implies, involves Ilorin housewives. They gather into groups (according to age, compound, religious and social organizations) during ceremonies and go round to sing for celebrants and guests who in turn give them money. Except in religious organizations like the Alasalatu group, there is no fixed lead singer to this type of *waka*. Any member can lead if she has fine voice. The Housewives occasionally dance during the performance. It is not, however, an active dance like that done to oral songs like Dadakuada and Ere Baalu in Ilorin.[24]

The Housewives *Waka* artists only gently move parts of their bodies to the rhythmic patterns of the songs. Most of the time, they just sing without dancing. They greet any generous gift with an applause of "Owoo! Heee!" The housewives usually wear same type of clothing, called *Buba, Iro* and *Iborun*, in various colors, styles, tyings, and wrappings. At times members of social groups in the Housewives *Waka* wear similar colors! In a given ceremony there can be several such waka groups, and each comes around to perform their *waka*. This also adds color and shows uniformity within the same of the groups. The Housewives *Waka* is unlike both the Group *Waka* and the One-man *Waka*, where every artist puts on a big gown or a *buba* and a cap he likes.

Yoruba Muslim women from the southwestern part of Nigeria, in imitation of the Ilorin Housewives *Waka* form musical groups. Unlike the Ilorin waka, however, they add drums, *sekere*, and other musical implements to their *waka*. They include incantations and use songs from traditional Yoruba lineage poetry. They employ what the Muslim scholar of Ilorin would call hyperbolic and foul poetic statements characteristic of Ijala hunter's poetry, It must be said that the Ilorin Muslim scholar is always anxious to dissociate *waka* from Yoruba traditional performers of Ijala, Esa and the type. Apart from the praises showered on Prophet Muhammad and the prayers for *waka* patrons, the only other contents of Ilorin *waka* are humor and what I call matrimonial poetics: the discourse of social relationships within the Ilorin family house, especially among cowives and between wives and husbands.

The main innovation, which cuts across all types of Ilorin *waka*, was the introduction of microphone instruments used to further amplify their songs to listeners near and far. Group *Waka* artists use standing michrophones, while the One-man and Housewives *Waka* artists use portable loudspeakers.

One innovation, which was seriously resisted by the Ilorin audience and other Ilorin *waka* artist, was the introduction of a real drum – the *Iyaalu*, to Group *Waka* by Alhaji Wahabi Titilope Okelele, a hitherto *waka* lead singer. He was condemned for polluting the Islamic oral genre. As Labeka and Ruka further elaborated on in separate interviews,[25] Okelele's critics, among whom they belong, consider that this particular type of drum accompaniment would divert listeners' attention from the socioreligious messages of *waka*, which, they insist are most cogent in the *waka* genre.

WAKA: PERFORMANCE IDEOLOGY, AND ISLAM

The formalist ideology of art for art sake has no place in Ilorin *waka*. It is an art for the sake of God. It attacks behavior and acts considered contrary to the dictates of the social, moral, and political ethics in Islam. The Ilorln *waka* poets do not, like Izevbaye and Palmer, describe the formalist literary ideology, see art as that which just addresses the problems of sleeping soundly, that of live and let live.[26] The *waka* poets do not fertilize their artistic vision with abstract human thoughts outside the reach of or not relevant to their audience, with abstract moral values of an abstract religious pietism.[27] Their artistic worldview is informed by the need for what Chidi Amuta calls "dialelctical reconstruction and complete upheval of the decadent status quo."[28] Ilorin *waka* artists of the Dodo, Labeka, and Abisodun tradition represent what we may call Shaikh Abdullahi Dan Fodio's revolutionary school,[29] which is against the bastardization of Islam as being reactionary, dogmatic, and spiritually enslaving that does not allow for dynamism and realism.

Saddened by the socioethic rotteness of the society, *waka* poets, in an effort to effect immediate change, sound notes of warning to political, social, and religious leaders. They often assure them that no cheating can ever go without being punished. The following rendltion is a vivid example of the poets' message:

> Mo lokan tingbe o si nijo alakhira
> Okan tingbe o si nijo alakhira
> Eso fosika wipe ko'fika sile.
> Rere nio maa se mase saida
> Boti wu ko pe to yio pada labo o
> Okan tii gbe osi nijo alakhira.[30]

I said nothing goes unpunished in the hereafter
Nothing goes unpunished in the hereafter
Warn the cheats to desist therefrom
Always carry out good acts, not bad ones
However long you pepetuate your cheating, the
consequence shall catch up Nothing goes unpun-
ished in the hereafter.

The *waka* poets take up the political and religious elites
in the community who think their Arabic/Islamic and or
Western education has given them a higher status and therefore a passport for oppression and suppression of people and
for perpetuation of sociopolitical and moral evils in society.
The poets believe that the elites are ignorant as long as they
do not practicalize the true educated person's ethics of justice,
fair play, equality, and respect lor human rights, in their ways
of llife. The following *waka* songs do not mince words at all:

Eni o kewu akelo loni o kewu
"Inna akaramakum inda llahi ati kaa kum"
Eni okewu akelo leni o kewu
Kilanfani kewu teru o ba loo
Eni o ke wu akelo leni o kewu
Eni o kewu akelo leni o kewu
Ima amalo ninbe fun Lukumanu
Lo fi gbade, ninu awon anabi
Enio kewu akelo leni o kewu[31]

It is the [Islamic] educated person who practice
good ethics that is educated
"Verilly the noblest of you in Allah's sight is the
most righteous"
It is the [Islamic] educated person who practice
good ethics that is educated
What is the use of education that is not evident in
the behavior of the bearer!
It is the ([Islamic] educated person who practice
good ethics that is educate
It is the [Islamic] educated person who practice
good ethics that is educated
Education and practise were what Lukman had

That was why he was blessed among the prophets
It is the [Islamic] educated person who practice
good ethics that is educated.

At a point, the *waka* poets even tell politioal office
holders that their chances are only for today, and they might
be kicked out tomorrow. They must not become money and
power drunkards who, overnight, corruptly enrich themselves, celebrating their ill-gotten riches while the downtrodden and the vocal voices languish in hunger and in jail.
"Tomorrow," according to the *waka* poets, the masses, or
at least, a new set set of leaders would takeover the office
and hence, today's leaders may be made to account for their
ill-gotten wealth. Labeka makes these messages clear in the
following songs:

> Ola o di tenikan, ada biru e
> Bo ni ba n be lowo re,
> Dakun yo ni won
> Ola o di tenikan, adabi ru e.[32]
> Tomorrow shall be for other sets and they become
> leaders like you are
> If today is on your hand
> Do please watch your excesses
> Tomorrow shall be for other sets, and they become
> leaders like you are today.

The Ilorin *waka* artists demystify religious and traditional
leaders' sole claim to wisdom and to authority in the society.
As was characteristic of the late Mallam Aminu Kano[33] during
his political campaigns, *waka* poets quote from the Glorius
Qur'an in their political poetic compositions. They thus expose
these political cheats by letting the poor masses know, in the
Ilorin downtrodden's most cherished communication form,
that Allah does not make any human being the sole authority
over life and death. The following song is a good example:

> Ara to ba wu kaluku koda
> Ara to ba wu kaluku koda

Be da ba n serere
Abo inbo leyin o
Ara to ba wu kaluku koda
Eni tin sayida, abo nbo leyin o
Ara to ba wu kaluku koda
"Wa man ya'a mal misqala sharratin akhairan yarahu
Wamman ya'a mal misqala sharratin sharran yarau"[34]

Whatever manifesto wished by a person, let him
/her perpetuate
Whatever manifesto wished by a person let him/
her perpetuate
He who perpetuate goodness
Good reward would soon catch-up with him
Whatever manifesto wished by a person, let him/
her perpetuate
He who perpetuate wickedness Nemesis shall
soon catch up with him,
Whatever manifesto wished by man, let him/her
perpetuate
"Whoever does good, however small shall have
goodness after him/her [as reward]
Whever does evil, however small, shall have evil
after him/her. "

The *waka* poets conscientize the members of their audience
about their rights being denied them and about how to stand
up to demand those rights. Their songs, which include quo-
tations from Qur'an and references to Islamic history, make
people realize that political power is a trust from the people
and from God; that any leader who abuses his office should
cease to enjoy good followership and obedience from the
masses. In a public performance, the following *waka* poet
challenges his audience:

Loni, ta lo le se bi seyyidina Abubakar, mo bere
ni?! Ato lori, ati mekannu? Abubakar se ijoba pelu
iberu Olohun. Ko sare fafa, ko bere susu nitoripe
o fe je olori. Nigbati won yan Abubakar lolori, o
so fun gbogbo al-humma annabi, oni: "Iseyi te
yan misi, ko kin se emi ni mo dara ju ninu gbogbo

145

yin. Oni, ti mo ba see re, ti mo se gege bi ofin Olohun ati Annabi Muhammad se la kale, e tele mi, efi owo sowopo pelu mi. Gbara ti mo ba bere si daaru, ti nfi ara niyin, ti in tele t'olohun ati ojise re, ke fun mi ni imaran, tin bagbo, e pada leyin mi, edite, e gbogun ti mi, e gba ijoba lowo min." Abubakar lowi be. Olori wo lo le so be loni? Eniyan wo lo le gbogun ti olori ni toripe ko se ijoba pelu ilana ofin?[35]

Today, who can behave like our leader Abubakar?! I have asked you, who among our current leaders and the poor followership can do this? Caliph Abubakar led wiith the fear of God. He was not desperate for position of leadership. When Abubakar was chosen as the head of the Muslim nation, he told all the citizens, he said: "The job you have chosen me to perform, it is not that I am the most suitable of you all. If I perform it well, if I perform in line with the law, in line with the prescription of God and His Apostle, Muhammad, follow me; join hands with me. Immediately I deviate [from performing well] and start to make life difficult for you and cease to follow the injunctions of God and his apostle, criticize me. If I refuse to heed your advice, withdraw your support of me, rebel and declare war against me, sieze power from me!" It was a Caliph of Islam who said that. Which leader in our contemporary society can say that? Who among the people can declare war on a leader when he ceases to rule according to the rules of law?

The *waka* lead singer does not only recall a true Islamic history but also invokes its spirit to mobilise the people against the present-day corrupt leadership inn his community. For one, he informs the audience that a leader must obey laid down laws that seek social justice, equality, and fear of God. He also makes the people realize that they must take an oath before assuming office, and that such an oath must recognize the right of the led to withdraw their obedienee immediately when the leader becomes power drunk. The poet's last two questions are rhetorical. They are challenging the masses to stand up and be ready to declare war against bad leaders.

We must identlfy here the recognition of both leaders and the people of Ilorin and indeed, in Nigeria as a whole, of the dialectical relevance of *waka*, especially the great passion and respect the Ilorin audience has for it. Already, the early 1990 Nigeria national campaign project MAMSER[36] and the Ilorin traditional leadership are hijacking it as a tool for the mobilization of people for their programs. Often times, *waka* songs are on radio advertising government and MAMSER activities. Also, in a fund-raising ceremony organized by Ilorin Descendants Progrersive Union, tagged the Ilorin Foundation, *waka* poets were employed to perform in all nooks and crannies of Ilorin Emirate to mobllize people for the launching. At the grand finale of the launching, for example, the following *waka* song was rendered throughout Ilorin:

> Gbogbo ara Kwara esare wa
> Gbobo ilu Kwara ni won ke si
> Gomina wa, Alwali Kaziri,
> Atoba Sulu, At'oloye yoku
> Niwon se maran, wa da lonsin si le o
> Gbogbo wa yanyan kati Kwara leyin o
> To rawa lagba latun jedikota
> K'ilu Kwara ko le lo siwaju.[37]

> All you people of Kwara, come here quick
> All the communities in Kwara State are called upon
> Our Governor Alwali Kaziri,
> And the Emiṛ Sulu, and other title holders
> They decided and organized the (fund) launching
> All of us must support Kwara State
> Because we (Ilorin areas) are the elder ones, also the headquarters
> So that Kwara State can progress.

CONCLUSION

George Thompson is quite correct when he contends that the poet speaks not for himself only but for his fellow people.[38] The poet's reality is demonstrated by the Ilorin Waka poet. The waka poet boldly practices his belief that "his cry is his people's cry, which only he can utter."[39] (parenthesis mine). The Ilorin *waka* artists, especially the Group Waka artists, must continue to address social issues and to highlight threats to justice and freedom, since it is "part of the very legitimacy of their poetic undertaking."[40]

Waka poetry confirms that even without musical accompaniments, oral literary production can still produce the desired effect. The critical mind is stimulated, and the excessive emotional feelings derived from enjoying the music and drumming is checked. F.M. Deng[41] is right in his strong contention that a good song should be capable of moving the audience "toward its objective." If the objective of a revolutionary song is to stir up passive people from a perpetual state of inertia, it may be important that such a song be devoid of too much pomp and pageantry that the drum and the dance provide.

Afterword

There is no doubt that globalization means many things to Africa and its Diaspora, and the first segment of the twenty-first century will show wether Africa, in particular, takes its place as an equal player in the global century or wether it is sidelined as a dumping ground for global gabbage. Despite the internationalization of African cultures—for example, hip-hop, albert emanating from the New World to almost every nook and cranny of the globe—continues to carry new languages and forms as it changes to new models. The *real deal* for peoples of African descent has been the retention of the spirit behind this globalized African performance form rather than the ownership of the global capital emernating from the performance culture. Which is more important: The fact that hip-hop artisits are millionaires or the spread and influence of hip-hop around the world? Perhaps what globazation has brought us are more questions than answers and more complexities than simplicities. I do hope that this book has presented ways to ask these questions from a position of knowledge where Africa and its Diaspora are concerned.

The electronic technology of this century so far seems to know only European (and lately Asian) languages and still does not seem ready to catch the fire of an African tongue. The more gadgets and mathines manufactured to ehance human performance in the global age, the less they fit into the cultural nuances of Africa and its globalized peoples. The more the people of Africa in seaerch of greener pastures migrate to the West, or recently in perhaps neglible numbers to the Asia Tiger countries, the less they are able to hold on to their linguistic and cultural forms, the less they are able to rcongize themselves as Africans. Yes, the name Africa perhaps continues to follow them every where they go, but in most cases a name is like an empty shell if it is devoid of its cultural contents such as indigenous languages and other traditional nuances. The plurality that enabled the countries of Africa, and indeed many parts of the non-European world, to allow European languages and, social and cultural forms to prosper on its soil since colonization is now being subjected to riddicle in the new global dispensation. I hope this book has been able to show that there is a different form of plurality and of multiculturality that is more credble, one that I strongly believe is better suited to the contemporary world and one in which every person and nation retains the pride and the content of their own indigenous culture. I strongly believe that it is this type of plurality and multiculturality that our world currently desires as the global village. The question, however, is whether this would ever materialize in the West!

If it did there would be a continued formation of global pluralism in the West defined only by faces of immigrants. This is not because Westerners are in love with immigrants' faces. They enjoy the cheap labor that immigrants provide Western farms and factories. Africa's economic posperity and that of the less developed nations would dwindle. The question is would it dwindle even further in the twenty-first Century as the migration of people from South to North increase? As the influence of the already mighty Western corporations continues to rise in Africa and around the world, poor peoples from the exploited nations would troop off to the West in the hope of a better social and economic posperity, whch the Western corporations and their local regime collaborators made impossible for them in their own coutries.

As the influence of the electronic superhighway and its twenty-four-hour broadcast cycle into Africa grow, it might become very difficult for people on the continent to recognize their own children, who would be covered more in Western robes and speak more in tongues popularized by the Western electronic media. While the case in Africa and other exploited areas of the world may be inredeamable without major counteractions in child and adolescent and higher education and in other cultural policies to protect the people from the "evils" of the Electronic Age. An avenue to change the status quo of pluralism and multiculturalism in the New World may already be in motion, especially in the United States.

I foresee the possibility of "new global century immigrants" defined by the sheer power of population (power of numbers!) forcing a change in the comcept and practice of Western pluralism. This will be brough about because of the immigrants' continued attachment to their indigenous languages, to their native homes and cultural origins, and to their increased political and economic power in their new countries. Again, the new immigrants' constant stretch to retain access to their home cultures, to retain their indigenous languages, and to remain regularly involved in the affairs of their native homes to the extent enhanced by affordable transportation and electronic access will cause a real change in the nature of the plurality of the West. A new census projection has actually shown that Latinos will eventually overtake the white population in the United States. The new Latino immigrants would vote according to those interests and very soon such a vote would be decisive in chosing political leaders in the United States!

Endnotes

Chapter 1

1. Here I refer more to the use of words, the construction of sentences, and the pronunciation.

2. See "Some Thoughts on Traditional Hausa Aesthetics and Arabic Influence on Yorùbá and Hausa Written Traditions in Nigeria," chapter 3 of my book, *African Discourse in Islam, Oral Traditions, and Performance* (Routledge, 2009).

3. I must emphasize that my own understanding of being a Muslim is not antagonistic to being a cultured African person (see my paper "Is *Al-Mukhlit* a Critically Useful Term for the Islamic Features in African Literature?").

Chapter 2

1. Discussions in the next four paragraphs are versions from my "The Influence of Traditional Oral Poetry on Modern Religions (Islam and Christianity) among the Yoruba (Nigeria)," *Frankfurter Afrikanistische Blätter* 6: 65-74.

Chapter 3

1. See Samuel Johnson, *The History of the Yorubas* (Lagos: C.M.S., 1921), 7.

2. See Herold Courlander, *Tales of Yoruba Gods and Heroes* (New York: Crown, 1973), 21.

3. See also S.F. Nadel, 1942, 1954.

Chapter 4

1. I identified this earlier at the end of Chapter 3 as one inter-prepation of Lou Dobbs's treatment of the immigrant's language.

2. The peace agreement between the Sudanese government and the Sudan People's Liberation Army (SPLA), which ended the longest armed confict in Africa in 2005, led to the formation of a national unity government and granted Southern Sudan a six year autonomy, to be followed by a referendum about independence. (http://en.wikipedia.org/wiki/Politics_of_Sudan. Accessed on 7/5/2009).

3. I have discussed the name Yoruba in chapter 2.

4. I prefer to avoid the word dominant in this case.

5. I prefer to leave the words in continuous tense.

Chapter 5

1. See my book, *Africanity, Islamicity, Performativity: Identity in the House of Ilorin*

Chapter 6

1. It may now begin to seem less "civilized" to refer to oneself as "ethnic"!

2. Edmonton is the capital city of the Province of Alberta, and was made up of about 800 thousand people in 1997.

Chapter 7

1. Telephone interview with Dr. Lesley McCullough by the author on 27 April 1998.

2. I didn't ask her whether the tutor was white or black. The emphasis here is on her gender.

3. Telephone interview with Dr. Lesley Mccullough on 27 April 1998.

4. My wife, who had practiced as a doctor in the St. George's General Hospital in Grenada for about six months, then told me that colonial influences continued strongly in all spheres

of Grenadian life. She explained to me the unique flavor of the Grenadian form of English, and the initial problems I might face understanding some Grenadian pronunciation of English in what she called the Grenadian accent.

5. This is a long traditional dress most popular among the Hausa of Nigeria. My own had some embroidments, as is common on such dresses in Nigeria. I was also wearing a cap y called Shagari cap during the second republic Nigeria.

6. This is a long traditional dress most popular among the Hausa of Nigeria. My own had some embroidments, as is common of such dress in Nigeria. I was also wearing a cap popularly called Shagari cap that was popular during Nigeria's Second Republic.

Chapter 8

1. President Mathieu Kérékou's open letter was posted on an online list-serve by Wole Soyinka where Africanists were debating the recently released documentary by Henry Louis Gates Jr., "Wonders of the African World."

2. It was widely reported that King Jaja of Opobo was among the African Kings who vehemently ressted slavery and was removed from the throne by the white slavers and exciled to where he violenty died.

3. Part of this song was recalled for me by Rahmat Olohuntoyin NaAllah.

4. My transcription from "Wonders of the African World" PBS Home Video, 2000.

5. Joseph E. Inikori, Professor of History, University of Rochester, was among the contributors to the "Wonders of the African World" debate on electronic list serve, moderated by Toyin Falola, 2000. He expressed this opinion during that online debate. These online debates have been compiled into two series of the online journal, *West Africa Review* (http://www.westafricareview.com/), vol. 1, No. 2, and Vol. 1, No. 2a.

6. Toyin Falola, in a private e-mail discussion with me on my contribution to the online debate, 2000.

7. Wole Soyinka, contributing to the "Wonders of the African World" debate, 2000.

7. Ali Mazrui's contribution to the list serv debate, 2000. The Nigerian historian he cited was Ade Ajayi.

8. Named after Benjamin Whorf and his hypotheses regarding the relation of language to thinking and cognition and for his studies of Hebrew and Hebrew ideas, of Mexican and Mayan languages and dialects, and of the Hopi language. ("Whorfian hypothesis." *Encyclopædia Britannica*. 2009. Encyclopædia Britannica Online. 06 Aug. 2009 http://www.britannica.com/EBchecked/topic/643031/Whorfian-hypothesis).

9. To "commit death" here does not mean committing suicide or killing himself. The Elesin Oba will not use any object to kill himself or strangle himself. Nobody will kill him. The act of committing death described here cannot be called suicide either. For want of a different explanation, it might be said that he wills himself to a different life in order to serve as a companion of his king to the ancestral world. He will, through dance, music and rtituals, go into a spiritual and metaphysical trance and into "death" in order to accompany his king to the word of the ancestors.

Chapter 9

1. A. Na'Allah, "Arabic and Islamic Education in Ilorin" *Unilorin Pedagogue*, 1985, Vol. II, p. 37.

2. Ibid.

3. N. Skinner. *A Grammar of Hausa*. (Zaria: Northern Nigeria Publishing Company, 1977).

4. A. Na'Allah, "Arabic and Islamic Education" p.37.

5. S.U. Abdullahi, *On the Search for a Viable Political Culture*. (Kaduna: New Nigerian Publishing Company, 1984) pp. 10–20.

6. A. Na'Allah, "The Effects of Poetry on the Religious Life of Ilorin," *The Phoenix*, Vol. 1, No. 1, pp. 19-25.

7. R. Finnegan, *Oral Literature in Africa*, (Nairobi: Oxford University Press, 1970), p. 53.

8. It is a commmon Qur'anic school's songs in Ilorin up till now. I remember having sung at *yisihi* Wolimat as a child.

9. A. Na'Allah, "The Effects of Poetry..." pp. 10–20

10. Alhaji Labeka, Oral Interview, Idiape Ilorin, 8 September 1990.

11. Ibid.

12. A. Na'Allah, Oral and Performatic Arts..." p.9.

13. Ibid.

14. See M. Parry "Studies in the Epic Techniques of Oral Verse - Making I: The Homeric Language as Language of an Oral Poet" 1930 and A.B. Lord, *The Singer ot Tales* (Harvard: Harvard University Pres), 1967.

15. Isa Olorin, "Wake Artist "Field Performance" Adabata, Ilorin, 25 Septenber 1990.

16. A.S. Musaffereddin *Ninety Nine Names of Allah* (Lagos: Islamic Publication Bureau, 1yto).

17. There is a whole chapter in the Holy Quran, "The Chapter of Unity," dedicated to preaching the oneness of Allah. It says Allah is one, has no son and was not born by anybody.

18. Bayo OgunJimi has always made it clear in our discussions that the achetypal pattern of sacrifices in all world religions usually meant appeasing the gods or goddesses to seek their favors, referencing the idea that god is a spollt child who needs to be pet to listen to the creatures – Bayo Ogunjimi, University of Ilorin, 1986-1 990.

19. Alhaji Adebimpe, *waka* Artist, Field Perfortance, Oke-Apomu, Ilorin, 17 May 1989.

20. AlhaJi Labeka, Waka Artist, Field Performance, Ile-Imam, Agbaji, Ilorin, 5 December 1989.

21. Rukayyat Sularana, Waka Artist, Field Performance, Ilorin~ November 1990.

22. Ibid.

23. Ibid.

24. See A. Na'Allah, "Dadakuada: Trends in the Development" pp. 97-113.

25. Alhaji Labeka, Oral Interview, Idiapa, Ilorin, 8 September 1990. Rukayyat Sulemana, 27 October, 1990.

26. C. Amuta, *Theory of African Literature* (London: Institute for African Alternatlves), 1987, p.21.

27. Onoge, "Toward a Marxist Soclology of African Literature" *Ife Studies in African Literature and the Arts.* No.2, 1984, pp.7-8.

28. C. Amuta, The Theory of African Literature, p.18.

29. Shaikh Abdullahi Dan-Fodio has been identified to be very revolationary. He always preached uprightness and complete compliance to Islamic ideas. He had to protest at times when his ideas were suppressed. It is atill believed that Shaikh Abdullahi's revolutionary ideas were always suppressed during and after the Sokoto Jihad, because of the fear of its truth and revolutionary effect. See S.U. Abdullahi, *On the Search for a Viable Political Culture.*

30. Alhaji Labeka, Waka Artist, Field Performance, Ile Imam, Agbaji, Ilorin, 4 December 1990.

31. Ibid., 5 December, 1989

32. Ibid.

33. Malam Aninu Kano, the leader of NEPU and later PRP (in the Nigerian Second Republic) the main political opposition parties with stronger based in Nigerian Republic Northern Nigeria. Chinua Achebe and Wole Soyinka were ntembers of PRP.

34. Adelope Pakata, Waka Artist, Field Performance, 1 September, 1989.

35. AlhaJi Labeka, Waka Artist, Field Performance, Ile-Imam Agbaji, 5 December, 1989.

36. Mass Mobilization for Social Justice and Economic Recovery (MAMSER) was set up by the Babangida Administration in 1985 to mobilize Nigerians for the revamping the Nation's economy.

37. Ibid., Waka Artist, Ilorin, 6 November, 1990.

38. Thompson, Marxism and Pottrv (New York: International Publishers, 1946), p. 6.5.

39. Ibid.

40. Amuta, *The Theory*, p.177.

41. Francis Mading Deng, *The Dinka and their Songs* (Oxford: Clarendon Press, 1973) p. 93.

158

Bibliography

꿔꿔

Aarne, Antti Amatus. *The Type of the Folktale: A Classification and Bibliography*. Trans. and enlarged by Stith Thompson. Helsinki: Suomalainen, 1961.

Abimbola, Wande. *Ifa Divination Poetry*. New York: Nok Publishers, 1977.

Abrahams, Roger D. *Deep Down in the Jungle: Negro Narrative from the Streets of Philadelphia*. Chicago: Aldine, 1970.

Abu-Laban, Baha. "Multiculturalism and the State Ethnic Policies in Canada." In *Status and Identity in a Pluralistic Society*. Edited by P. Krishnan. Delhi: B.R. Publishing, 1995.

Achebe, Chinua. *Things Fall Apart*. London: Heinemann, 1958.

Ahmad, Khurshi, ed. *Islam: Its Meaning and Message*. London: The Islamic Foundation, 1980.

Alao, Jaigbade. Field Performance. Popoigbonna, Ilorin, Nigeria, 1987.

Ali, Abdullahi Yusuf. *The Holy Qur'an: Text, Translation and Commentary*. New rev. ed. Maryland: Amana Corporation, 1989.

Amao, Omoekee. "Field Performance." Ile Alhaji Raimi Iyanda, Omoda, Ilorin, 1987.

Amster, Randall, "Arizona Bans Ethnic Studies and, along With it, Reason and Jutsice" in *The Huffington Post*, http://www.huffingtonpost.com/randall-amster/arizona-bans-ethnic-studi_b_802318.html, posted on December 29, 2010, 12.08pm. Accessed on January 14, 2011.

Andrews, L. William. "The Beginnings of African American Literatures." In *The Oxford Companion to African American Literature*. Edited by William L. Andrews and Francis Smith Foster. New York: Oxford University Press, 1997.

Ang, Ien. "On Not Speaking Chinese: Postmodern Ethnicity and the Politics of Diaspora." *New Formations* 24 (1994): 1-18.

Angus, Ian. *A Border Within: National Identity, Cultural Plurality, and Wilderness*. Montreal: McGill University Press, 1997.

Appiah, Anthony Kwame. *In My Father's House: Africa in the Philosophy of Culture*. New York: Oxford University Press, 1992.

_____. "Reconstructing Racial Identities." *Research in African Literatures* 27 (1996): 68-72.

Appignanesi, Richard, ed. *Cultural Studies*. Cambridge: Icon, 1997.

Apter, Andrew. "The Pan-African Nation: Oil-Money and the Spectacle of Culture in Nigeria." *Public Culture* 8 (1996): 441-66.

Aremu, Odolaye. "Shehu Shagari Geri Ijoba." Ariyo Sound A SSLP 058A, 1979.

Awolalu, J. O. *Yoruba Beliefs and Sacrificial Rites*. London: Longman, 1979.

Awolalu, J. O., and P. Dopamu. *West African Traditional Religions*. Ibadan: Onibonoje, 1979.

Adepoju, Lanrewaju. "Oro Oluwa." LALPS 142, 1990.

Babalola, A. "The Characteristic Features of Outer Form of Yoruba Ijala Chants" *Odu* 1 (1964): 20-42.

_____. *The Contents anf Form of Yoruba Ijala*. Oxford: Oxford University Press, 1966.

Badejo, Diedre L. "The Yoruba and Afro-American Trickster: A Contextual Comparison." *Presence Africaine* 147 (1988): 3-17.

Baughman, Ernest Warren. *Type and Motif Index of the Folktales of England and North America*. The Hague: Mouton & Co., 1966-67.

Beier, Ulli. *The Return of the Gods: The Sacred Art of Suzanne Wenger*. Cambridge: Cambridge University Press, 1975.

Ben-Amos, Dan. *Sweet Words: Storytelling Events in Benin*. Philadelphia: Institute for the Study of Human Issues, 1971.

Bilgrami, Akeel. "What Is a Muslim Identity? Fundamental Commitment and Cultural Identity." *Critical Inquiry* 18 (1992): 821-42.

Bissoondath, Neil. *Selling Illusions: The Cult of Multiculralism in Canada*. Harmondsworth: Penguin, 1994.

Breton, Raymond. "Canadian Ethnicity in the Year 2000." In *Multiculturalism and Intergroup Relations*. Edited by James S. Frideres. New York: Greenwood Press, 1989.

Brown, William Wells. *The Escape; or A Leap for Freedom. Black Theatre USA*. New York: The Free Press, 1974.

Burnet, Jean. "Taking into Account: The Other Ethnic Groups and the Royal Commission on Bilingualism and Biculturalism." *Multiculturalism and Intergroup Relations*. Edited by James S. Frideres. New York: Greenwood Press, 1989.

Chinweisu, et al. *Decolonization the African Mind*. Lagos: Pero Press, 1987.

Chowdhury, Kanishka. "Afrocentric Voices: Constructing Identities, (Dis)placing Difference." *College Literature* 24.2 (1997): 35.

Clark, J. P. *The Ozidi Saga*. Ibadan: Ibadan University Press, 1977.

Courlander, Harold. *Tales of Yoruba Gods and Heroes*. New York: Crown, 1973.

Cruikshank, Julie, Angela Sidney, Kitty Smith, and Annie Ned. *Life Lived Like a Story*. Vancouver: University of British Columbia Press, 1990.

Deng, Francis Mading. *The Dinka and their Songs*. Oxford: Clarendon Press, 1973.

Douglass, Frederick. *The Education of Frederick Douglass*. Hermondsworth: Penguin Books, 1995.

Eades, J. S. *The Yoruba Today*. Cambridge: Cambridge University Press, 1980.

Euba, F. *Archetypes, Impecators and Victims of Fate*. New York: Greenwood Press, 1989.

Fadipe, N. A. *The Sociology of the Yoruba*. Ibadan: Ibadan University Press, 1970.

Finnegan, Ruth. *Oral Literature in Africa.* Oxford: Oxford University Press, 1970.

_____. *Oral Poetry.* Cambridge: Cambridge University Press, 1977.

_____. *Oral Traditions and Verbal Arts: A Guide to Research Practices.* London: Routledge, 1992.

Fontenelle, M. de. *Conversations on the Plurality of Worlds.* Berkeley: University of California Press,1990.

Forde, Daryll. *The Yoruba-speaking Peoples of South-Western Nigeria.* London: International African Institute, 1951.

Fowke, E. *Canadian Folklore Ontario:* Oxford: Oxford University Press, 1988.

Fowke, E., and C. H. Carpenter, comps. *A Bibliography of Canadian Folklore in English.* Toronto : University of Toronto Press, 1981.

Frazer, J. G. *Anthologia Anthropologica: The Native Races of Africa and Madagascar.* London: P. Lund, Humphries & Co., 1938.

Freud, S. *Two Short Accounts of Psychoanalysis.* Hermondweller: Penguin, 1962.

Frideres, James S., ed. *Multiculturalism and Intergroup Relations.* New York: Greenwood Press, 1989.

Gates, Henry Louis. "Wonders of the African World." PBS Home Video. 1999.

_____. *Wonders of the African World.* New York: Alfred A. Knopf, 1999.

_____. *The Signifying Monkey: A Theory of Afro-American Literary Criticism.* New York: Oxford University Press, 1988.

Gbadegesin, Segun. *African Philosophy: Traditional Yoruba Philosophy and Contemporary African Realities.* New York: Peter Lang, 1991.

Gleason, Judith. *Orisha: The Gods of Yorubaland.* New York: Atheneum, 1971.

Goldenberg, Sheldon. "The Acquisition and Transformation of Identities." *Multiculturalism and Intergroup Relations.* Edited by James S. Frideres. New York: Greenwood Press, 1989.

Graham, W.A. *Beyond the Written Word: Oral Aspects of Scripture in the History of Religion*. Cambridge: Cambridge University Press, 1987.

Grimm, Jacob, and Wilhelm Grimm. *Kinderth-und Hausemärchen*. Stuttgart: Reclam, 1980.

Heminghway, Ernest. *The Old Man and the Sea*. Paris: Gallimard, 1952.

Hermon-Hodge, H. B. *Gazetteer of IlorinProvince*. London: Goerge Allen, 1929.

Idowu, Bolaji. *Olodumare*. London: Longmans, 1962.

Ikeda, Hiroko. *A Type and Motif Index of Japanese Folk-Literature*. Taipei, Taiwan: Orient Cultural Service, 1983.

Imam, Sa'adu. Personal Interview by author. Ilorin, Nigeria. 1987.

Jackson, Bruce. *"Get Your Ass in the Water and Swim Like Me": Narrative Poetry from Black Oral Tradition*. Cambridge, Massachusetts: Harvard University Press, 1974.

Johnson, Samuel. *The History of the Yorubas*. Lagos: C.M.S., 1921.

Labelle, Huguette. "Mulitculturalism and Government." *Multiculturalism and Intergroup Relations*. Edited by James S. Frideres. New York: Greenwood Press, 1989.

Lado, Robert. *Linguistics across Cultures: Applied Linguistics for Language Teachers*. Ann Arbor: University of Michigan Press, 1957.

Lévi-Strauss, Claude. "The Structural Study of Myth." *Journal of American Folklore* 68 (1955): 428-44.

Lord, Albert B. *The Singer of Tales*. Harvard: Harvard University Press, 1960.

Mazrui, Ali. *The Africans: A Triple Heritage*. Boston: Little, Brown, 1986. (Also in video.)

McCullough, Lesley, "On Her Visit to Malawi." *Midday Express*, produced by Bred Harris. CBC Radio One, Alberta, Canada, 14 April 1998.

_____. A telephone interview with Lesley McCullough, by Abdul-Rasheed Na'Allah. Alberta, Canada, 27 April 1998.

McGary, Howard. "Alienation and the African American Experience." In *Theorizing Multiculturalism*. Edited by Cynthia Willett. Boston, Massachusetts: Blackwell, 1998.

Na'Allah, Abdul-Rasheed. "The Influence of Traditional Oral Poetry on Modern Religions (Islam and Christianity) among the Yoruba (Nigeria)." *Frankfurter Afrikanistische Blätter* 6 (1994b): 65-74

_____. "Muslim Women and Ilorin Traditional Oral Poetry." *The Literary Griot* 7 (1995): 101-12.

_____. "The Origin of Egungun: A Critical Literary Appraisal." *African Study Monographs* 17, no. 2 (1996): 59-68.

_____. "Interpretation of African Orature: Oral Specificity and Literary Analysis." *Alif: Journal of Comparative Poetics* 17 (1997b): 125-42.

_____. Introduction to *Ogoni's Agonies: Ken Saro-Wiwa and the Crisis in Nigeria*. Edited by Abdul-Rasheed Na'Allah. Trenton: Africa World Press, 1998.

_____. "Is *Al-Mukhlit* a Critically Useful Term for the Islamic Features in African Literature?" Presented at the Modern Languages and Comparative Studies Graduate Students Conference. April 1998. Edmonton, Alberta, Canada.

_____. "Orality as Scripture: Verses and Supplications in an African Religion." In *The Transformation of Nigeria: Essays in Honor of Toyin Falola*. Edited by Adebayo Oyebade. Trenton: Africa World Press, 2002.

_____. *Africanity, Islamicity, Performativity: Identity in the House of Ilorin*. Bayreuth: Bayreuth African Studies, 2009.

Nadel, S. F. *A Black Byzantium: The Kingdom of Nupe in Nigeria*. Oxford: Oxford University Press, 1942.

_____. *Nupe Religion*. London: Routledge, 1954.

Naipaul, V. S. *Beyond Belief: Excursions among Converted Peoples*. New York: Random House, 1998.

Nelson, Harold D., et al. *Area Handbook for Nigeria*. Washington, D.C.: U. S. Government Printing Office, 1972.

Neufeldt, Bradly. "Cultural Confusions: Oral / Literary Narrative Negotiations in *Tracks* and *Revensong*. Master's thesis, University of Alberta, 1997.

Norman, Howard A. Ed. and trans. *The Wishing Bone Cycle: Narrative Poems from the Swampy Cree Indians*. New York: Publishing Company, 1976.

Ogunjimi, Bayo, and Abdul-Rasheed Na'Allah. *Introduction to African Oral Literature*. Ilorin: Unilorin Press, 1991.

Ojaide, Tanure. *Poetic Imagination in Black Africa: Essays on African Poetry*. Durham, North Carolina: Carolina Academic Press, 1996.

Okpewho, Isidore. *The Epic in Africa: Toward a Poetics of the Oral Performance*. New York: Columbia University Press, 1979.

_____, ed. *The Oral Performance in Africa*. Ibadan: Spectrum, 1990.

_____. "Introduction: The Study of Performance." In *The Oral Performance in Africa*. Edited by Isidore Okpewho. Ibadan: Spectrum, 1990.

_____. "The Oral Performer and His Audience." In *The Oral Performance in Africa*. Edited by Isidore Okpewho. Ibadan: Spectrum, 1990.

_____. "Towards a Faithful Record: On Transcribing and Translating the Oral Narrative Performance." In *The Oral Performance in Africa*. Edited by Isidore Okpewho. Ibadan: Spectrum, 1990.

_____. *African Oral Literature*. Bloomington: Indiana University Press, 1992.

Olajubu, Oludare. "Iwi: Egungun Chants in Yoruba Oral Literature." Master's thesis,

Olajubu, Oludare, and Abdul-Rasheed Na'Allah. "Omoekee Amao: A Legend of Yoruba Folksongs" *Sunday Herald*. Ilorin, Nigeria, 4 December 1988, pp. 5-6.

Olatunji, Olaitan Olatunde. "Characteristic Features of Yoruba Oral Poetry." Ph.D. diss., University of Ibadan, 1970.

Olaoye, Raimi A. "The IlorinEmirate and the British Ascendancy 1879-1918: An

Overview of the Early Phase of IlorinProvincial Administration," Master's thesis, University of Ilorin, 1984.

Olokun, Oloye Idowu. *Imole -Aye*. Oke-Eso, Ilesa: Nigeria, n.d.

Ong, Walter. *Orality and Literacy*. New York: Methuen, 1982.

Osundare, Niyi. "How Post-Colonial Is African Literature?" In *Caribbean Writers: between Orality and Writing*. Edited by Marlies Glaser and Marion Pausch. Amsterdam and Atlanta, Georgia: Rodopi, 1994.

Probyn, Elspeth. "Technologizing the Self" In *Cultural Studies*. Edited by Lawrence Grossbeg, Cary Nelson, and Paula Treichler. New York: Routledge, 1992.

Rassner, Ronald." Narrative Rhythms in a Giryama Ngano: Oral Patterns and Musical Structures." In *The Oral Performance in Africa*. Edited by Isidore Okpewho. Ibadan: Spectrum, 1990.

Rose, Peter I. "American Ethnicity in the Year 2000." *Multiculturalism and Intergroup Relations*. Edited by James S. Frideres. New York: Greenwood Press, 1989.

Scheub, H. "The Technique of the Expansible Image of Xhosa *Ntsomi*- Performances." In *Forms of Folklore in Africa*. Edited by Bernth Lindfors. Austin: Texas University Press, 1997.

Schmidt, Nancy J. "Recent Films by Sub-Saharan African Filmmakers, II" *ALA Bulletin* 24 (1998): 2-9.

Schwarz, Frederick August O. *Nigeria: The Tribes, the Nation*. Cambridge: MIT Press, 1965.

Seitel, P. *See So That We May See: Performances and Interpretations of Traditional Tales from Tanzania*. Bloomington: Indiana University Press, 1980.

Sekoni, Ropo. "The Narrator, Narrative-pattern, and Audience Experience of Oral Narrative Performance." *The Oral Performance in Africa*. Edited by Isidore Okpewho. Ibadan: Spectrum, 1990.

_____. *Folk Poetics: A Sociosemiotic Study of Yoruba Trickster Tales*. Westport, Connecticot.: Greenwood Press, 1994.

Shaw, Thurstan. *Nigeria: Its Archeology and Early History*. London: Thames, 1978.

Soyinka, Wole. *Death and the King's Horseman*. London: Methuen, 1975.

_____. *The Open Sore of a Continent: A Personal Narrative of the Nigerian Crisis*. New York: Oxford University Press, 1996.

_____. "Telephone Conversation." In *A Selection of African Poetry*. Introduced and annotated by K.E. Senanu and T. Vincent. Harlow: Longman, 1988. University of Lagos, 1972.

_____. "The Yoruba Egungun Masquerade Cult and Its Role in the Soceity." *The Masquerade in Nigerian History and Culture*. PortHarcourt: University of PortHarcourt, Nigeria. 1980.

_____. *The Voice of the Artists: The Voice of the People*. Twenty-eight in the Series of Inaugural Lectures. Ilorin: University of Ilorin, Ilorin, Nigeria, December 1987.

Tedlock, Dennis. "On the Translation of Style in Oral Narrative." *Journal of American Folklore* 84 (1971): 114-33.

_____. "Learning to Listen: Oral History as Poetry." In *Envelopes of Sound*. Edited by Ronald J. Grele. Chicago: Precedent, 1975.

_____. *Finding the Center: Narrative Poetry of the Zuni Indians*. Lincoln: University of Nebraska Press, 1978.

Thompson, Stith. rev. *Motif Index of Folk Literature*. Bloomington: Indiana University Press, 1955.

_____. *European Tales Among the North American Indians: A Study in the Migration of Folk-tales*. Arn Arbor, Michigan.: University Microfilm, 1970.

_____. *Types of Indic Oral Tales: India, Pakistan, and Ceylon*. Helsinki: Suomalainem, 1960.

Ting, Nai-tung. *A Type Index of Chinese Folktales*. Helsinki: Suomalainem, 1978.

Tunstall, Kate E. (Ed.). *Displacement, Asylum, Migration: The Oxford Amnesty Lectures* (Oxford Amnesty Lectures): Oxford: Oxford University Press, 2004.

Yai, O. "Issues in Oral Poetry: Criticism, Teaching and Translation." In *Discourse and its Disguises: The Interpretation of African Oral Texts*. Edited by K. Barber, P. F. de M. Farias. (Birmingham U African Studies Series.) Birmingham: Centre of West African Studies, 1989.

Willett, Cynthia, ed. *Theorizing Multiculturalism*. Massachusetts: Blackwell, 1998.

Zumthor, Paul. *Introduction Å la poásie orale*. Paris: Editions du Seuil, 1983.

Index

Hausa 3-5, 7, 9, 17-20, 24, 43, 55, 56, 64, 66, 89, 91, 93, 97, 119, 123-125, 130
Heritage Day 87
Hip-hop 149

Idowu 65
Ifa divination 6
Igba 18
Igbo identity 62, 63
Ijoba 61, 77, 145, 146
Ijoba eleyameya 61
Ilorin identity 43, 63
Indigenizing difference 69
Indigenizing process 67, 70
Indigenizing similarity 67
Individual personality 87
Indonesian village 106
Iran 61

Jaja, King 110, 116, 117
Johnson, Samuel 17, 19, 21, 23, 24, 35
Jonathan, Goodluck 10

Kanuri 56
Katunga 17-19
Kérékou, Mathieu 110, 121
Kincaid, Jamaica 100
Kwa 22

Labelle, Huguette 85, 86
Lado 4

Law 18, 52, 53, 77, 81, 82, 102, 146
Laye, Camara 9
Legal immigration 84

McCain, John 82, 83
McCullough, Lesley 95, 96, 104, 106
Muhammad, prophet of Islam 120, 125, 128, 136, 139-141, 146
Muhammed, Prophet 124, 129
multicultural codes 1

Na'Allah, Rasheed 60, 91
National identity 76, 78, 86, 87
Nativization process 66
Nativizing difference 70
Nilo-Saharan 22
Nobel Prize 8, 16
noncybersocieties 1, 2

Obama, Barack 14, 49, 50, 52, 83
Ogunde 43
Olaiya, Moses 43
Olajubu 34
Olaoye 66
Olatunji, Olaitan 34
Ologun ijala 44
Ong 2, 7
Ooni 56